MW00792019

Persecuted

But

Not Forsaken

By

Kenneth M. Lee

My Life as a MK-Ultra Victim

Persecuted But Not Forsaken by Kenneth Marshall Lee.

Printed and bound in the United States of America. All composition rights are reserved; Material included herein shall not be used for commercial intent; neither shall it be reproduced for or within information storage and retrieval systems.

Copyright © 2021

ISBN 9780971185012

About the Author: Kenneth Lee is a free-lance author who lives in Loris, South Carolina, U.S.A. His devotions have been published in *The Loris Scene, The Upper Room, Penned from the Heart, and The Secret Place*

He self-published four devotional books: *God's Help Now!; God's Divine Help; Devotions A-Z*, and yearly devotional booklets, Qu*iet Heavens*. In 2022, he published his first fiction novel, *Victim's Vengeance.*

His *Petition to Cease and Ban Direct Energy Programs and Surveillance of Humans* in 2004-06 brought together a group of covertly abused victims to seek justice and relief.

*When excerpted, Bible Scripture References are from the King James Version and the New Schofield Reference Edition of the Holy Bible.

Foreword

The events in this story are true to the best of my knowledge and recollection; however, some of the names have been changed, other than my parents, who deserve vindication. Any relation to the fictional names in this story is purely coincidental and unintentional.

Dedication

This Book is dedicated to my family, both past and present, who never knew how, why, or who persecuted them.

My mother and father were simply trying to live the American dream by having children, good jobs, and a safe place to live.

But their lives would be targeted to fail at no fault of their own.

To all the victims of electronic targeting, stalking, forced drugging, sadistic sexual abuse, and character defamation, God counts the tears and will have vengeance on our attackers.

Table of Contents

Spring 1980, Norfolk, Virginia

Spring is in the air, with forsythia bush flowers turning yellow and dandelion flowers covering the ground.

Winter's cool air from the Chesapeake Bay begins to wane as warm humid southwest winds blow across the Southeast United States from the Gulf of Mexico.

The temperate air invites me to go jogging.

I have been running periodically for a year now to relieve stress from the green monster at work. The green monster is a mechanical mail sorting machine that stretches out to 75 feet long by 12 feet wide, with a chain driven carriage inside that drops mail into keyed destination area bins.

I am expected to key the first three digits of zip codes every second for forty-five minutes with a fifteen minute break, in which I go to the back of the machine and load mail from the bins into trays and gurneys, or, to the front of the machine and load mail on each of twelve conveyor belts for the other operators.

By the end of the night, I felt like I've been through a meat grinder, not only from being around the rattling chains of the machine but the stress of being audited.

An operator must key at 95% efficiency, and the supervisor can audit anytime.

Fall asleep while keying, and the un-keyed mail will fall into a bin near the supervisor's desk, only to be returned to an embarrassed operator.

So I often run in my spare time, mostly in the mornings, because I work in the evenings.

Sometimes I enter five mile and ten-kilometer races on the weekends, but I have not placed in the top ten or even the top twenty-five; yet it feels good to get exercise.

This morning, I put on my sweat pants, tennis shoes, and a T-shirt and went outside to enjoy the spring weather and run about three miles.

It's a quiet neighborhood where I live, with several dead end streets and little traffic.

One mile into my run I jumped a guardrail off Military Highway. When I came down, I felt pain.

I ignored it for awhile, but when it got worse, I slowed to a trot, and eventually I had to walk.

Arriving home, I limped through the front door entrance. I knew something bad had happened to my leg.

Doris, my wife, did not show any sympathy; she said nothing as I complained about my leg. I hobbled to the chair in the kitchen and sat down.

The next day, I visited an orthopedic doctor. Dr Young said, "You have torn your quadriceps muscle that is just above the left knee."

"Will it heal?" I asked.

He said, "Sure, in time. But for now it's bed rest and patience. Make an appointment to see me in two weeks."

But after a couple of weeks there was no relief from the pain, and the doctor suspected there was another problem, so he sent me to Dr. Levy, a nerve specialist at the Medical Tower in downtown Norfolk.

On the appointed day, I got to the car by using some crutches I had found at the Salvation Army store.

I drove to the Medical Tower in downtown Norfolk. I exited the car and entered the old yellowed brick medical building that overlooked The Hague – a dirty tributary of the Elizabeth River that has gathered filth from the shipyards and is yet one of the most beautiful spots along the Ghent section in Norfolk. Ghent, at the time, consisted of old wooden three storied houses with large porches and banisters that overlooked cobblestone streets.

Suspicious of doctors, I hesitantly opened the door to Levy's office.

There was no secretary, but he soon came out from an adjacent room with a file of papers in his hands.

Levy checked my knee for reflexive action by tapping in the front of it with some instrument.

He turned around and scratched his head as if something else was on his mind, and then went to his desk and began to write.

He explained that I had some kind of nerve damage right at the top of the left thigh but he didn't know the full extent of it; so he scheduled me to see some specialist from South Carolina.

In a couple of weeks, the specialist arrived and hooked up a bunch of wires to my body and began her tests. Weeks later, her report indicated there was damage to my left femoral nerve, but Dr. Levy said the nerve would regenerate in time.

For now, I could not put any pressure on the left foot.

I wondered how this nerve injury could have happened from jogging; so one day, I went back to the Medical Center again and its library on the first floor. I wanted to find out about the nerve problem.

I discovered that stress from standing could be a factor, and I did a lot of standing at the Post Office when I was not on the machine – casing magazines and newspapers into cardboard trays.

I found Marines often suffered femoral nerve injuries from standing in the same place for extended periods of time.

Well, there it is, I thought. *It is because I have to stand for long periods of time when I'm not on the machine.*

But the book also said the nerve will regenerate in most cases.

So my therapy began; and every day I moved my leg back and forth as Levy suggested, but I felt nothing, and in fact, the muscle began to atrophy.

3

Sitting lame got my attention towards God.

Jesus said, "I am the resurrection, and the life; he that believeth in me, though he were dead, yet shall he live;" John 11: 25.

The words startled me, yet filled me with comfort and hope.

My spiritual life had been dead for so long and now something was different: I had been humbled.

But there was definitely something else going on in my life --I just couldn't figure it out.

I began to listen to Pastor Dr. Vernon McGee's *Through the Bible Radio* broadcasts on the radio, and that helped me somewhat.

Since then, he has passed into the heavens. Fortunately, a series of *Through the Bible* books have been published.

Searching for something to do, I ordered some crafts from a New England store and began constructing stools. After putting the stools together, I would cane them with rush, cane, or reed splits.

It was very comforting, but my life would take a new direction one warm sunny afternoon while sitting on my southern porch caning.

A stranger approached me with a Bible in his hand.

A meek looking fellow with glasses on his face and dressed in a suit, he calmly walked up to the porch and introduced himself as a member of the neighborhood Presbyterian Church; and he gave me an invitation to come on Wednesdays and Sundays.

I wasn't quite used to someone being so kind. For one thing, I had been spending most of my time working in a fast paced mail processing environment, and I wasn't sure what was going on with Doris.

I obliged and said I would try to attend as soon as I felt better.

After three months of not being able to walk, I woke up one day with some feeling in my thigh -- and finally in my foot.

The nerve was regenerating, and the muscle which had completely disappeared, started returning.

Then, I was able to stand up for a couple of seconds, and I could even hop around and put a little weight on my left foot.

As long as I walked briskly, I could walk. And so I walked, and walked, and walked.

A month passed and I worked my way up to walking a mile, but I still couldn't stand up over thirty seconds in the same place.

But it didn't matter. The important thing was I stood up. And now my spiritual life was beginning to flourish.

One hot and humid night in September of 1981, I walked up to a nearby Baptist church and found the doors open.

I walked inside and found no one present but the doors to the sanctuary were open, and the light from the foyer that illuminated the aisle in the front of the altar invited me to come.

I meekly walked to the front, laid on the floor, and poured out my emotions and heart to God. And there was a silence in heaven, just as the Bible describes.

And then I saw the angels descending with Christ on the right side, and there was a great peace, as I had been converted to another person, just as what the Holy Spirit does when repentance from sin takes place in front of a holy God.

I had found my life, and shortly thereafter I would find truth, as bad as it would be.

It had happened unknowingly sixteen years prior, and then I began to understand.

1965 – Twelve Years Old

I had suffered earaches early in my childhood but nothing like the one I had on a Sunday morning in 1965 when mom was in Richmond marrying an old friend.

Of course, now I know it was all planned by the perpetrators to have me at home alone.

It was no big thing about me being alone -- I was used to that, but I hardly expected someone to sneak into my bedroom in the middle of the night and needle me with radiological sensitive toxins in my Eustachian tubes to try and control me the rest of my life.

I called mom that Sunday morning at the hotel's number she had left.

"I need to talk to my mom, Merle Lee."

"There's no one here by that name," the operator said.

Holding my ear in pain, I hung up the telephone.

I looked at the number again. It was the one I had just dialed, and then I remembered she may have checked in with her new husband's name Wade.

So I called back, and the operator made contact and connected me to their room.

"Mom, my ear hurts terribly."

"Well, put a warm cloth on it," she had said, "and the pain should go away."

"Tried that but it's still pulsing terribly," I said.

"Try it for awhile longer and call me later if it still hurts."

"Okay. Sorry to bother you," I said.

The pain did not go away, and I had to call mom again. She couldn't get home until Tuesday then she would take me to Doctor Schechner.

This is just what my attackers wanted – me to be implanted and mom's marriage weekend to be spoiled.

6

I know now what those black things are that dotted Dad's face.

People called them blackheads, but those blackheads are substances that absorb radiation and stimulate the nerves when energized.

Mom finally did get home and took me to the doctor, but the ear oil he gave me did little good --it was not getting rid of silicone implants.

I lay on the bed for days unable to concentrate for any amount of time, with the right side of my head swelling.

Had I known the Central Intelligence Agency was busy initiating a program named MK-Ultra that targeted 36,000 unwitting victims including Native Americans with involuntary drugging, stalking, remote sensing applications, and electronically sensitive implants to try and manipulate their behavior, I might have screamed to someone and got relief.

But I was a victim, and still am.

This is the conclusion I have come to after talking with other victims and finding black toxin polymer carbon based substances in my body and being stalked for years.

Waking up paralyzed in the back of my pickup truck one morning while parked at a fishing pier somewhere around the year 2004 only encouraged me to find who, what, when, where, and why someone was trying to disable and kill me.

I did not ask to be put in this targeting program -- I was obviously born into it, and I will not keep silent about the most torturous, debilitating, and murderous act upon the earth in the history of mankind.

I'd much rather be fishing, sitting at home with a wife or friends, or writing about the principles of religious redemption.

Many other victims feel the same way, but some have also suffered immensely, such as Cynthia Goldman, who was murdered in her home, Pam Anderson pleaded for help from the government bio-ethics commission only to receive none. After she left Washington, D.C., she went back to California and killed herself.

And then there's Clare Werhle, who died in a hit and run accident in Florida, shortly after she said her CIA boyfriend was responsible for her targeting.

There have been countless victims who have been murdered.

But something is obviously different about me, for I've escaped twelve direct murder attempts: four auto collisions, poisonings, and covert injections.

These perverts have spent an inordinate amount of time on me! Not to mention including the military using aircraft throughout the country to harass innocent folk under the guise of training programs. Many victims have testified of this activity taking place.

Possibly this survivor trait of mine comes from my Indian heritage. Maybe it's from God Almighty who visited me on that hot humid September evening in front of the altar on that dimly lit church aisle.

I don't know, but after I received a new life that day in the church aisle in 1980, I now testify about my life so other people will understand the targeting process.

Yet, the program goes on.

When I realized I could not fight the perpetrators alone, and shortly after I was implanted in the parking lot at the Emerald Fishing pier, I went home and wrote a petition to get people together. I knew there were other victims out there somewhere: I just had to find them.

My *Petition to Cease and Ban Direct Energy Programs and Surveillance of Humans* in 2004 gathered 600 signatures over three years.

Not a whole lot of signatures you might think, but nearly each individual was a very special person who had suffered immensely.

You might ask, "Why don't you just go to a lawyer and get justice?"

For one thing, the legal community is scared to death to initiate a suit against intelligence agencies of the U. S. Government for fear they may get targeted. And some lawyers have been targeted.

I think of one recently in Florida who testified about being attacked by microwaves. Failing to recant her testimony, her license to practice law was suspended.

The targeting frequencies are such that any lawyer, juror, or judge could easily be influenced to disregard legal precepts.

A couple of victims I understand have had some success in filing complaints against the perpetrators, and more cases are finally being certified.

But some litigants in the past were simply put under a gag order to keep the targeting secret.

This remote targeting can affect anyone, anywhere, in any situation. And now I understand implants aren't needed to stimulate a person's nerves. Every nerve in the human body can be stimulated by a certain radiological frequency, but the implants do make it easier, being placed in special nerve centers to be remotely activated. And there are natural transmitters in the blood.

But anyway, I personally saw five legal firms close office in the Va. Beach area or move shortly after I visited them in a two-month span around 1989 when I was trying to get a second opinion about a couple things in a divorce case (a case which had also been programmed – the real estate agent's name was "Cas-on").

I knew right then this targeting issue wasn't just a local issue; it was global with technical surveillance designed to shut down the slightest bit of truth gathering evidence against public officials. (My wife's attorney was a State Legislator.)

Now this targeting is widespread over communities to cause people to be angry at one another, commit terrible acts of violence, and live nomadic lives in fear and loneliness.

The perpetrators want their victims to run to doctors, counselors, lawyers, and other professionals for help, rather than seek an all knowing God who provides truth, mercy, and compassion.

The Bible says, The fear of man bringeth a snare: but whoso putteth his trust in the Lord shall be safe (Proverbs 29: 25).

I suppose obeying that doctrine has kept me alive, for when trouble came, I simply found the quietest area and prayed to God for help.

I knew divine protection was available because Mom was always reciting proverbs to me.

I've listed scripture readings throughout this book, at the very times I needed something to rely on for guidance, truth, and comfort.

The scriptures have been my only comfort in life. Growing up with parents who were targeted -- and never said they loved me or expressed moral support, lead me to find alternative sources, in which case were to read the scriptures. Certainly I thank mom for guidance on that.

The scriptures actually helped me understand the targeting process: how Jericho fell without a shot being fired, how the devil is constantly looking for human sacrifices to atone for sin rather than accept the death and resurrection of Jesus Christ, and the numbering system he utilizes with computers to target people.

Attendance at a Presbyterian church only encouraged me to learn more about the scriptures.

Visiting professors from the nearby Christian law school would often preach about archaic languages and give much insight to the Spirit of God.

I do thank God for Reverend Leon Wardell, who prayed for me daily, for years.

Unless non-ionizing radiation is regulated such that the human nervous system will not be disturbed, there are going to be some terrible things that happen in the future. Of course they already are with all the mass shootings.

The Beginning

I was born May 22, 1953, in Norfolk, Virginia, at DePaul Hospital, which was located a few blocks from the Elizabeth River.

From what I have been told, it was a very hot and humid summer.

It makes me wonder if that's why I returned to the eastern coastal region of the United States fifty years later after spending twenty years in the mountains, because I like humidity.

My family had just arrived from St. Paul, Minnesota, where they had raised my brother James for nine years.

Jobs were plentiful in Norfolk because of World War II taking place, and the U.S. Navy had bases in the Hampton Roads area where skilled workers would be needed to maintain ships and aircraft.

That brought federal money into the area and stimulated the economy.

Not only was the Navy in Norfolk, but private maritime commerce was active at the International Loading Ports, with foreign freighters from counties all over the world visiting and delivering goods.

Jobs were a factor in my parents coming to Norfolk, but mom's sister, husband, and kids were also here.

But to give a little history about my parents is dutiful for this book.

My mother was born on the Cherokee Indian Reservation, in the Great Smoky Mountains National Park, in a little area called Smokemont.

There's a campground there now, where many of the natives from that region gather every year to socialize and tell of old times; then they go to an old wooden clapboard church around the corner for a good old foot stomping service.

"My mother's gone to heaven, and now I want to go. My father's gone to heaven and now I want to go."

Over and over parishioners would sing this hymn, all to the beat of shoes tapping on the wood floor with the sound reverberating throughout the hills on both sides of the church.

After being run out of Norfolk, with a helicopter following me to the State Line, I would get a job working for the National Park Service in this same area, maintaining the campground.

Mom had four sisters and two brothers, and they lived in a little cove in Cherokee where a little stream winded its way down from Rattlesnake Mountain from the east.

A spring on the opposite side of the road gave the family water for bathing and drinking.

When mom and I would come to Cherokee in the summers, I would visit the little spring and drink the cool water from a pipe that protruded from the rocks. It extended over an old rusty wash tub that continually overflowed with water, until one of my cousins thought the tub was attracting too many drunks and cut down trees blocking the trail.

The old people call the water "medicine water "– because it was on the north side of the hill.

It gets cold on that Branch where mom lived; the sun doesn't show itself over the eastern side of the hill until about 10:00 in the morning and sets about 4:00 p.m. even in the middle of summer. In the meantime, there is fog to burn off around the branch.

Mom and her brothers and sisters were sent for some time to the Cherokee Indian Boarding School at Smokemont.

It was one of many schools where the whites started to try and mold Indians to the white person's way of

13

thinking. Certainly, the Cherokee Indian language would no longer be taught.

A smart girl, mom was allowed to skip the third grade and go the fourth.

I have little other information about mom's history because she never talked much. For one thing, she was programmed to be quiet.

That's what the programming does, it keeps a person from relaxing and sharing life with other people, not only in fear of being tortured more but being accused of having mental illness if the words come out slurry or conversation suddenly becomes confused.

Mom was suspicious of everything, so the less said the better I suppose, but I have learned some information from my Aunts and others.

From what I've heard, mom met my father, Robert Lee, at the Fontana Dam construction site area of North Carolina about 1941. The dam was about fifteen miles from Cherokee and there was work there. Mom waited on tables at a local eating establishment and dad was a cook.

I don't know what dad was doing in that part of the country, other than wanting to fish: he loved to fish.

Dad was from Iowa, but he did like to cook and fish and I suppose that's how he ended up at the restaurant at the dam.

Dad was born in 1922 in West Union, Iowa. Dad's mom died shortly after his birth; she was only 35 years old, and if I might add, the only smiling person in a group family portrait of twenty-five Lees. She must have been an angel.

Dad was raised by his step-mother Rachel.

Dad's father was originally a farmer but eventually but got a job as a treasurer in Fayette County.

Grandpa was also a 33rd degree mason, and he died in April of 1962.

I'll not forget the funeral because mom and I took the long trip by plane to Waterloo, Iowa, on a dark stormy rainy night. The plane rocked severely and I hit my head on the roof.

Certainly, before the family torch would be passed, I would die in this plane. Fortunately, we landed safely.

But anyway, back to the 1943 era.

Mom and dad married and moved temporarily to Washington D.C., where my brother James was born in 1944, which I now believe was a forced move.

This was a time of World War II and many German doctors in the U.S. were experimenting with psychological behavior on unwitting victims.

My family's behavior would be manipulated for the next fifty years– whether because of my Cherokee mother or the nobility of my father's people.

The Lee family tree has an insigne topped off with the words: *Not Unmindful of the Future.* I suppose that means there is a continual fight for freedom and cry to be relieved from oppression.

Richard Lee, the first Lee to America, was known as the immigrant, and he was a very rich tobacco farmer and later the attorney general of Virginia.

Anyway, two Lees were signers of the Declaration of Independence: Richard and Henry.

Shortly after James was born in Washington, D.C. in 1944, the family moved to St. Paul, Minnesota. .

And then I came along at a very strange time after they moved to Norfolk.

When Dad died, I found out the circumstances of my birth.

It was in a dark unlit closet where I found a postcard from my mom stating that said she wasn't quite sure about him yet.

The card was dated September 1952, and the postmark was from Cherokee, North Carolina.

I stared at the card for minutes wondering if what I just read was real.

Not sure about him yet? They had been married near ten years.

Mom's writing further said, "I think I'll stay here for awhile. I'm not sure about you yet and I have to look out for my safety."

But that's not what really bothered me. This was the very month of my conception into the world!

I was born in May of 1953, and as later I would find out, the beginning of a very evil Central Intelligence Agency program labeled MK-Ultra, supposedly the MK meaning "mind- kontrolle" and the "ultra" standing for ultra capacitor, which I assume to be a microchip that stores and emanates energy via remote radiation.

I tried to compromise this card's message.

Oh, they had a little misunderstanding: they visited mom's family in Cherokee, made a little love at the Teepee Inn, and dad went to Norfolk to find work – and where Aunt Maude and family had already established themselves.

But the insecure words on the card would exemplify mom's life, and I know she was a victim of electronic targeting.

The manipulation techniques used by the CIA and other clandestine agencies, both domestic and foreign, are able to manipulate the lifestyle of an person, friends, family, and strangers. It is that concise and widespread, as many victims are now discovering.

Anyway, Mom and James eventually joined Dad in Norfolk and moved into the Lakewood subdivision near downtown. More room was needed when I came along, so the family moved into a house on Norvella Avenue in the Norview section.

James was about nine years old and on his way to meeting new girlfriends and participating in sport activities. He would star in track and baseball.

He hardly ever spent any time with me. He was too busy with his own life. I was on my own from the time I was a tot. But I can't remember hardly anything from 0-6 years old.

I do remember walking at least two miles in the morning to elementary school and back home. I wouldn't normally get home until 4:30 in the afternoon! Many times it would be dusk before I got home. I was never on time for class in the mornings.

Anyway, this was about 1959 and mother had a good telephone operator's job with the Chesapeake and Potomac Telephone Company. Dad worked as a route salesman for Mary Jane Bakery downtown.

I remember Dad's job because he would sit me on the hard metal floor of the truck and I could feel every bump on the road. Finally he showed mercy and gave me a wooden bread rack to cushion myself.

My life on Norvella Avenue consisted of exploring the local woods and spending a considerable amount of time walking to school and back.

But I don't doubt there was a reason the man next door to us operated a ham radio, as I discovered one day by accident when the missus invited us kids in for cookies and the old man was gone. Paranoid, you might think? Many victims have complained of ham radio emanations affecting their behavior after being implanted.

Suddenly it was time for us to move.

1959

Considering I needed to get closer to school, mom and dad bought a house in the Fox hall section of Norfolk.

Pine Ridge Elementary school would be only a mile away; the Baptist Church was less than a mile; and there were shopping stores nearby.

Mom would be within walking distance to her bus stop; so she could get downtown to work at her new job at the water department.

This was heaven for me, because in my isolation as a targeted kid, I could now go visit the bums in the community that were hanging around the shops off Princess Anne Road and get odd jobs.

The move inconvenienced James somewhat, because his high school was now four miles away; yet he had a car and could drive there.

Fox Hall and the four hundred acres of vacant land next door would become my playground for the next ten years.

Military housing had been there, but it had been torn down after the war was over. What was left were piling holes, cracked asphalt streets, and bent street signs.

I spent most of Sunday afternoons in the piling holes pretending they were fox holes -- as seen in the war movies where soldiers were hiding from the enemy.

I'd sit in the holes basking in the warm sun eating a pomegranate and watching planes fly in and out of the Norfolk airport, which was only a few miles away.

But I would also explore the land's perimeter ditches for turtles, snakes, and lizards. In those fields, I played with wild dogs and hunted rabbit traps for Mr. Harrison, who lived down the street and would give me 25 cents for each trap with a rabbit.

Pine Ridge School sat in the middle of this playground, and I did well there for six years, until I was implanted.

I was active in sports, flirting with girls, and excelled in my studies. I loved school, and I would arrive an hour early to play kickball or visit a janitor named Jones in the boiler room to get warm by the coal stove and get some wisdom.

The coal furnace would burn wildly with a dump truck load of coal sitting nearby.

Jones and I would smoke cigarettes, look at dirty magazines, and he would let me shovel some coal into the bin on occasion. Jones had sense, and I wanted to learn from him.

I loved older people, probably because my dad was never home and I was looking for elderly guidance.

I was a young vibrant kid who wanted to live life to its fullest. I could have done without the disciplinary action of writing 25 paragraphs of why I should not spit on the sidewalk, but I was a normal kid who did a few things contrary to the rules. Kissing a girl in the back room at the library also got me in trouble, but it was worth it.

I was also an obsessive reader, digesting adventure and spy stories.

Though I was supposed to be asleep at night, I'd sneak my rubberized little boy blue lamp and put it under the covers to read a book, until I fell asleep.

The light was very dim and probably why I could see so well in the dark, until my perpetrators injected something in me. I've heard the perpetrators use something to bother the optic nerve.

Now I know I was being groomed for something other than what normal American kids do, because I was reading a bunch of spy books.

But anyway, back to the new house. It was a Cape Cod style house with two bedrooms, a floor furnace, living room, dining room, kitchen, and a den with a lot of windows where Dad would make a little office for his new pest control business.

The windows often got busted out when a batter in the nearby field lofted a baseball over the perimeter hedgerow and into the house.

I remember the floor furnace distinctly at the house because my brother would push me off it when there was heat. But more often, there was no heat, because the oil drum would be empty.

The other thing I remember is crawling up in the attic and putting pots on the joists to catch rain coming in from the leaking roof.

There was a smaller adjacent two-acre field next to the house, where I spent much time playing ball, flying kites, and sleeping out with my buddies in a tent on hot summer nights. A hedgerow separated the field from the house, so we were protected from anyone seeing us smoke cigarettes or eating muffins we had pilfered from neighborhood bread trucks.

My journey into the world of thievery ended abruptly one night when my buddy John and I decided to pilfer cigarettes and loose change from a parked car.

As we were rummaging the front seat area, a large light shined directly on us from the porch. Sitting on the porch was an off-duty policeman who conveniently had some handcuffs for John and I. He threatened to take us to jail. He scared me enough that I gave up stealing forever after that, and I wish I could thank the man today. I believe his name was Mr. Cherry.

Other than those activities, I was playing Little League baseball, scouting the local woods for anything of value, and vainly kicking rocks along the path of a ditch on my way to the store or gas station.

I would on occasion be found on a nearby river riding on a friend's aluminum boat wondering if we'd ever get back after the motor sheared a cotter pin. This branch of the Elizabeth River was so filthy, but it was a path to freedom for us kids. Floating under a Virginia Beach Boulevard overpass made it even more exciting.

At nights, I would visit the ball fields in the park, which were built a couple of years after we moved to Fox Hall. I would watch the bruisers in the police leagues play softball.

Those activities, and my daily trips to the nearby drug store, which had a magazine rack and snack bar, kept me busy.

So I had settled into somewhat of a good life, but mom and dad were not, and our targeting would start in earnest.

The Targeting of the Family

I don't remember dad being at the house much after we moved to Fox Hall. I do remember us watching some television, him maintaining his office in the side room for his new business, and him and mom playing cribbage in the small dining area.

Other than that, my memories aren't much.

Dad had started a business and called it *Twin City Pest Control*

The programming puts many talented people into vocations such as pest control, plumbing sewage, janitorial, housecleaning, and nanny jobs – anything to keep a victim out of jobs that influence public opinion.

After him and mom separated, and the targeting had begun in earnest, he picked me up a couple of times and took me to his apartment at Chesapeake Beach.

Sometime around 1962, dad was poisoned when a waitress gave him household ammonia in place of ammonia spirits for a headache. His esophagus was burned and he would be fed through a tube for months.

I do remember visiting him in the hospital and seeing all the tubes hooked up to him.

In order to follow dad's programming, a similar thing would happen to me twenty-six years later – poisoned at 33 years old.

That's what the programming does: tries to get the kids to follow the actions of the parents and blame maladies on genetics regardless of personal character.

The perpetrators would do a similar thing to my daughter, sending her to school 1500 miles away from home, near a military base where I was stationed twenty some years earlier in Kansas.

For another example of programming, Dad had earlier cooked for a living, and cooking would be the one merit badge I would earn in the Boy Scouts. I really didn't have that much interest in cooking, but there I was cooking eggs and bacon for the group of scouts while on a camping trip.

About this time, my mother became paranoid; she did not trust the food in the house. And then mom stopped talking to her sister, who lived just six miles away.

Where before we would go over to my aunt's house every Sunday night to play poker, talk, and have fun -- all of that stopped-- because mom and her sister stopped talking.

It's difficult to understand mom filing for divorce at this time, because she was a believer in the Lord. She took me to church every Sunday, and she taught Sunday School.

But Dad was a womanizer, and obviously targeted.

About this time also is when mom got some land in Cherokee and she was included on the Baker roll.

She started working her way back home.

For what it's worth, her divorce lawyer's last name at the bottom of her decree was Abrahav. Years later, I tried to research this lawyer's name but found nothing on Norfolk's city register.

But I suppose it was Abraham. Like many lawyers who are ashamed of their filings or don't want to be known, their name suddenly becomes illegible.

But dad was popular with women, for he serviced restaurants and met quite a few women.

Maybe that's the reason mom filed for divorce, but she wanted financial security, and dad's business was not financially lucrative.

My brother, who was living with us at the time, along with his beautiful wife, began to feel stressed from his draftsman's job at a time when stress was not a household problem.

My brother quit his job and got some kind of compensation as a result. He was definitely targeted.

But anyway, I heard some kind of story the FBI was chasing my brother because he was involved in a shootout. He eventually landed in Memphis Tennessee, where he re-married a nice Christian woman and had a second child. He was awarded disability and would not work another day in his life as far I know -- choosing to play golf.

The last time I saw him was in a Cherokee Court meeting room when he threatened me shortly after I had filed a caveat to a copy of a testamentary will my mother had not signed: the original had been destroyed.

But anyway, around 1962, his first wife Carol got pregnant, and they moved out of the house into an apartment near my aunt.

I babysat my nephew for some time, and coincidentally found out years later, he was dancing in one of those skimpily dressed shows in New York.

But MK-Ultra is partly designed to make sex slaves out of its victims. Many a victim has complained of sexual attacks from electronic targeting. Manipulating the electro-magnetic fields around a victim to push the blood to sensitive areas will cause sexual stimulation.

The victims chosen are good looking, which reminds me of biblical characters such as Daniel and his friends, who were fair to look upon and enslaved to serve the king: they had no blemish and were intelligent.

It's my opinion mom's remote targeting started when she was a young girl on the Reservation. I have little doubt they took her appendix out for their purpose.

But she definitely started showing the signs of being targeted shortly after we had to moved to the house in Fox Hall on West Norcova Avenue, at the time of the

24

divorce, which would be an event the perpetrators would like to blame their activities on.

Many victims first think a particular incident has caused their targeting, but as time passes, they find the targeting had been from birth. And now, many victims find their targeting has been generational – going back to the initial colonization of America.

Because of mom's paranoia, and wisdom I might add, for dinner each night I would have to ride my bicycle up to a grocery store one mile away to get food.

I didn't mind, because I kept the leftover change, and I enjoyed traversing the sloped ditch behind the Turner's Express Trucking Company and continuing across neighborhoods to the grocery store.

Mom would hardly ever cook anything out of the refrigerator. That was a no-no in our targeted world: there was hardly ever more than three items in the refrigerator.

Mom stopped socializing with her sister and stopped working at her new job at the water department downtown. But did start working as a secretary with Colonial Stores credit union, which was actually closer to home.

Shortly after the divorce, mom met an old friend by the name of Howard Wade. Howard had a drinking problem, but he did work and bring home money, which is something we lacked for some time.

I never had more than three pairs of pants and a couple shirts, but this is also representative of the targeting. If I did acquire something nice, the perpetrators would put holes in it or make a tear. This wasn't too common in the first years of targeting but it escalated in the last twenty years.

This clothes tampering happens to nearly all victims.

My Targeted Adolescence

And this is when I was attacked and victimized as I explained earlier.

After the covert implant attack in my bedroom around 1965, I went from an absolutely outstanding student in 5th grade to mediocrity, loneliness, and problems with my health.

My summers were spent wandering the streets of Tidewater on my bicycle, going so far as to Virginia Beach on occasion and even Chesapeake Beach on two occasions. That was ludicrous! Seeing that they were ten miles from the house and the traffic in the Norfolk area was heavy.

But there in my targeted world, it was an escape – to load up my bicycle basket with a few snacks in the morning, tools for the trip, and take off for destination unknown.

Many times I would pedal the three-mile ride to the Airport, where I would catch turtles and ride the trails in the botanical gardens.

But I did have fun. And when the sun went down, I often loaded back up and ended my day at Norfolk International Park where the Triple-A Tidewater Tides played baseball.

The attack would destroy the best years of my life: I would suffer ten years of receiving subliminal music emanations to my head – songs that repeated themselves over and over. Worse, I became distracted easily and could no longer concentrate on my schoolwork.

My life would continue on its downward spiral. My school grades dropped. I couldn't make the transition to eighth grade at Lake Taylor Junior High School. And I had few friends.

Something wasn't right. I wasn't dumb, because I had outstanding grades all through elementary school. In the seventh grade, I still passed a test that put me in an accelerated math class program taking algebra a year earlier than everyone else. But I certainly wasn't capable of good grades with the targeting.

I knew I needed to go to work; so I got a newspaper route, and I started working at the local gas station. I suppose now this is what I was programmed to do: flunk school and go to work.

I loved the gas station however, and I got a lot of guidance from the old men hanging around there.

Here is where I learned to grease car fittings, change oil, and fix tires. I'd sweep off the service lot area, wash windows, and empty garbage cans. I'd be filthy at the end of the day but loved every minute of it.

I started off at 35 cents an hour. When I left the station at 17, I was making $1.25/hour. I was cheap labor for sure. But it was good for me. And then I could afford to buy my own food.

But now I understand why mom did not stock the refrigerator: there was the threat of poison. Dad would have never done such a thing, but the perpetrators would try and make it look like it because he was an exterminator.

I'm continually amazed to this day how a person can open their refrigerator and not give the least thought of something being drugged.

Nothing could be trusted at home. Still can't fifty years later.

Most electronically targeted victims claim perpetrators poison their foods if not only to induce physical sickness but accentuate the remote electronic targeting. If it had not been for my knowledge about activated charcoal neutralizing poisons, I'd be dead for sure.

Perhaps since you are reading this book, and you have started to put together events in your life that may have indeed been programmed. The first thing you want is stability. Well, check your food and make sure it's safe.

Then you want justice. Don't get angry, just start the pursuit to find out who, what, when, where, and how.

Were all these strange happenings to my family the products of divorce? Not hardly. The targeting of my family has begun in earnest. These perpetrators want to separate us and slow kill us -- which is what happened to all of us victims.

I was clued in one day when I tried to hook up my old bum friend George for a date with mom.

George may have dressed in rags, but George was smart: he was a former electrician at the Navy Yard.

A chain smoker originally from Kinston, North Carolina, he came up to Norfolk to get a job at the Navy yard like many people did during the war.

But George was anything but stupid. He had a 1953 Chevrolet in mint condition in his garage. He also had an old truck up until the time he got crazier. George was stockpiling silver quarters and dollar certificates long before anyone else ever thought about it. I saw his stash one day when he invited me into his house. Far as I know, I was the only person who ever had gone into George's secret quarters.

And I had seen him dress well on occasion, clothes far from his daily one-piece set of work overalls that had holes in them.

But George was a target. He had been under psychiatric care for years, and everyone in the neighborhood called him crazy George. I knew George was not crazy, from spending hours talking with him on the bench at the gas station and listening to his stories.

As my mother and George finished their first date, George talked about it the next day and said he enjoyed it, but he also said something I've never forgotten. "They are going to kill you and your mother."

I did not reply, but I knew George would not lie. I could only wonder about his statement however as the years passed. Now I know: the perpetrators and their technology have the power to make people say something with a forced speech program.

I've seen the patent on it, and I've experienced the continual pulsations to my neck and vocal chords.

Those of you who grew up in small towns and had close families may not understand how secret activities like these can happen, but when a family is in a large metropolis such as the Norfolk area, where there are a lot of covert agencies such as the FBI, CIA, Armed Forces Defense intelligence agencies, and God knows what other clandestine agencies and corporations exist including foreign entities, evil exists!

I mean, who knows what your neighbor is doing or where he works?

Or what about the milkman coming to your door? Or how about the diaper service guy coming to pick up the diapers

In the city, you learn to beware.

If the same covert involuntarily needling of my body had not occurred years later, I would have never figured out my family was being targeted.

But when I awoke one morning in the back of my pickup truck at the Emerald Isle fishing pier in 2004 to find the right side of my body paralyzed, I put the story all together. I could barely walk after this injection to my nervous system.

The perpetrators knew I was going there, and they knew I had figured out the targeting program. They knew I was going to take action to try and destroy it, because I was putting people together on the Internet with my petition.

After the attack, the next day, I visited another fishing pier in the same area. When I walked down the pier, a man who was sullenly smoking a cigarette with an arm on the wooden rail looked over at me and said, "I hear you've been having a little trouble."

I had never seen the man in my life, but obviously he had participated in the attack.

Junior High School

I made it through Junior High School on talent because I sure didn't study much.

I spent more time buying candies early in the morning at the drug store before the bus came to take me to school -- and sell them for a profit

I usually cleared 100%. Sweet-tarts, Jujubes, and an occasional candy bar would fill my bag to sell, and I would usually sell all.

Dad came back into my life about 1968 and tried to get me involved in a fraternity called The Knights of Pythias.

I hated the indoctrination process. It wasn't me to become involved with a bunch of guys that raised hell, drank alcohol, and partied all weekend. I was more like mom: quiet, reserved, intuitive, and a nature lover.

The first day of being a fraternal brother at Lake Taylor High School in the initiation process was too degrading for me, making me do pushups and carry other kids' books. I was already being degraded by my targeting; the last thing I needed were co-students harassing me. I think I actually finished the initiation process one night when they made me drink a quart jar of something ungodly. And then I got flogged.

I don't believe any of those actions prepared me for being a better person or enjoying fellowship: it reminds me of sadism, and the very actions I now fight against. But anyway, I participated in very little activities of the fraternity, choosing instead to be with my girlfriend Kathy.

I went with Kathy for several years in my teens and now I realized why I felt so comfortable with her in the

31

den at her parent's house: it was below ground and the electronic targeting couldn't get to me.

One other memory that I have that has been so prevalent was a shopping venture mom and I went on one Friday night after her work. Or maybe it was a Saturday. But anyway, the part I remember most was looking at and being able to select a race car set at a Sear's store, when I was about thirteen. So why is that etched on my mind?

It was below ground: I was less targeted.

What may have been a simple event to you reading this was a monumental one to me when I was free of electromagnetic targeting!

There have been certain geological areas where I felt free years later, but the perpetrators eventually covered those areas. One was the Nantahala Gorge in Western North Carolina, which was surrounded by cliffs. Another was a gap in the mountain near Cherokee. I could have stayed there for days enjoying the freedom.

About this time in 1969 Dad re-married, and I lived with him, Mary, and her son in Virginia Beach for a short time.

Her son David was real cool and would take me out at night in his Mustang, and he eventually became a pastor.

But he and dad really never got along too well.

While at Virginia Beach, I got a job at a high volume Texaco service station at Witchduck Road.

After the summer, I moved back home with mom.

To further complicate my life, forced school busing arrived in the city in 1970 and I would be bussed to Booker T. Washington High School near downtown Norfolk.

Looking at the dilapidated tilted bus with a near flat tire, exhaust smoke covering the road behind it, and students hanging out the windows made me want to turn around and go back home.

I attended Booker T. Washington High School for three days, and then I looked for greener pastures, I didn't need fighting on the bus, mayhem in the classrooms, and the weapons that were exhibited by the students; so I decided the State of Florida would be a better place to spend my time.

My friend Bill and I met in the parking lot of our old playground Industrial park one morning and we took off in my newly bought 1967 Pontiac Lemans to Florida.

We stayed for about three months, up until the time Brian was getting his pictures taken from a suspicious source I wanted nothing to do with, but I also got homesick for Kathy. However, I did have a good job in Daytona Beach working at a rest home bussing tables.

One good thing that happened on the trip was that we had stopped off in Myrtle Beach, and I enjoyed the laid back atmosphere. I doubt it's no accident I've made my home near there forty years later.

But anyway, when I got home, Mom was gone! There was no one at the house! And there were no signs of her living there!

The 3-6 Mark of the Beast

Mom had moved to another house at "1536" Cary Ave. She must have thought of me because it was a two bedroom home, and I could now go back to my regular school.

God cares about us even though we can't always see it, and I've come to realize this even in the most desolate circumstance.

But the three-six numbers such as the last two digits of the house address would plague my life for the next twenty years.

Phone, personal identification, license plate, access code, golf cart, plane, and hotel room numbers would be designated with a three and six or a combination thereof.

Now I know why: this is the devil's way of tagging people with computer program numbers to stalk, harass, and even kill people, all under guise of some kind of mark of the beast as described in the scriptures.

Here is wisdom. Let him that hath understanding count the number of the beast: for it is the number of a man; and his number is Six hundred threescore and six.
Revelation 13: 18

The MK-Ultra program started off with *36,000* victims.

Other victims have also complained about common numbers throughout their lives.

One female victim in Missouri had been plagued by fours and twos (which of course add up to 6). Her phone numbers, residence addresses, and other personal media would consist of fours and twos -- even her Social Security

Number. Other female victims also complain of the four and two targeting.

This all reminds me of when I got to South Carolina, where I looked at my electric bill only to see the account number ending in three-sixes.

My Social Security numbering adds up to or subtracts to the "six" digit all throughout; the phone number of a house where I would eventually start my own family in 1976 would be 461-6466, and the address was 6156.

The numerological pattern did not stop: Personal Identification Numbers would be assigned such as 6264.

In the Army, I would be assigned with a "36K20" Military Occupational Specialty Code – all products of a system designed to manipulate and control my life by technology.

I thought I'd get ahead of the evil number assigner the last time I went to the Division of Motor Vehicles to get a new license plate for my car by telling the clerk I wanted no sixes in my license number. She said she understood.

The three sixes are tagged to victims to make them identifiable. Now, my perpetrators usually have 3-6's on their car license plates. Some of them appear to be unwitting victims, and others have been blackmailed or paid.

The terrorist attack on the New York Trade Towers on 9/11/01 is a component of the three six targeting. The nine upside down is a six.

Just look at the numbers in the tragedies that have occurred in the last century – and you will see a pattern of three sixes, whether it be the date, address, plane flight number, number of people victimized, caliber rifle, etc .

Anyway, back to the Florida return trip.

I had not told mom I was in Florida, so I guess she didn't feel obligated to tell me she had moved.

I walked in the door of the house that morning October of 1970 to greet her, and without looking, she mentioned that breakfast was ready and to have some if I wanted.

Nothing else was said as she went off to work. That's mom, but the targeting does that.

There was nothing there for me in Norfolk.

So I decided to join the Merchant Marines. I went downtown to the Custom House and told the man I wanted to join, but they rejected me because I was 17.

Then I tried to join the Air Force. I told the man to give me any test and I would pass it, but he also declined saying I was not old enough.

I think both events were manipulated to try and get me to join the Army or Marines and die in Vietnam.

So I walked next door and joined the Army with my mother's signature on the enlistment form.

I had to do something; I was really unhappy with the school travel situation, and although I tried working for an electrical contractor, I just did not have the self-discipline to learn a trade at this point in my life.

Mom questioned my judgment about going in the Army while everyone else was trying to get out of the Armed Services and Vietnam, but I figured the war to be over soon and everything would be okay.

Just after Christmas, 1970, I got on a bus to travel to Richmond, Virginia for orientation and a physical examination.

We recruits were given some fine rooms at the Thomas Jefferson Hotel. And so we decided to party a little. We managed to find a couple of older guys to get us some beer. After that, we went exploring the hotel, which was magnificently furnished with plush red carpet, stone sculptures, and pictures of colonial America. Chatting with other guys who were facing the same rough odds, I was feeling life was great. I knew I had made the right choice to get away from home!

After a couple days, I and my new friend George, a black fellow from the Norview area in Norfolk, were off to Fort Campbell, Kentucky for basic training.

Thank God for George, because he got me back to the barracks one evening after a few drinks too many, and he gave me some great advice later in boot camp.

Sitting in a class one afternoon, the instructor informed me that I had one of the top three scores after general testing. That 118 point score qualified me to attend Officer Candidate School (118 I know now was just another product of the three sixes).

I was kind of confused on what to do. I'm not a person who likes to sit in the front seat, not that I can't handle it. But I'd as well be a humble little servant in a mighty castle.

I felt indecisive and looked over at George in the next seat.

"Well, what do you think George? I can be an officer."

"Don't do it, Ken," he said. "Those Second Lieutenants are the first ones on the front line in Vietnam."

"Oh. I figured there was a catch."

The instructor wanted an answer in thirty minutes, and I gave him one in thirty seconds.

"Not interested, sir. But thank you very much."

I know now the offer of OCS was another attempt to get me killed.

It was about six weeks before the drill instructors would let us go off base, and I took advantage of that weekend.

A few of us went into Clarksville Tennessee, had a few drinks and found our way to a movie. It was bitter cold that Saturday evening in February of 1971 as snow was falling and covering the streets of Clarksville. In the motel room, I felt lonelier than ever.

The next morning, I awoke to a foot of snow on the ground.

Across the street was a Baptist Church, so I decided to go. I felt I needed to go to church and was able to talk someone into going with me. The service would give me some confidence about life that I really needed.

Basic training never bothered me. I was always able to run well, endure cold temperatures, and get up early.

Many recruits weren't so lucky. They'd complain of frostbite on the rifle range, shortness of breath on long hikes, and lack of sleep.

Man. This was much better than living on the streets or a house with no one to help me.

The only thing bothering me was our instructors deciding our platoon was too fat; so they decided to cut down on breakfast and issue us one egg, a piece of bread, and a pancake.

I wasn't fat. I was only 159 pounds at 6 foot and I needed food. So I would prod the cooks in the mess hall to give me more.

The guy who bunked under me had a heck of a time. He was overweight and sweat would just drip off him even at night. He could barely breathe at times it seemed to me. He also had near flat feet and had a difficult time marching. They did finally give him some kind of profile that limited his participation. I would help him out and clean his rifle to keep him from getting in trouble.

But Basic Training got my attitude right.

I was marching along one day with my helmet cocked back like I always had it because it took a lot of pressure off my neck, and as any good hard working Asian person will tell you, balancing items is the way to carry them.

The drill instructor didn't find this philosophy too entertaining, and one day he came up behind me and slammed his hand down on my helmet jarring my head.

"Lee, I told you to get that helmet on right!"

Maybe he had warned me. I couldn't remember.

"Give me twenty trips around the platoon."

Now that will tire a man out while the platoon is marching.

I remember going out to the rifle range for a week or so in the most miserable weather of cold rain mixed with snow.

The visibility was awful with a fog that covered the area. The instructor would have us adjust our rifles for Kentucky wind and Tennessee elevation – but not fog.

The 300-yard silhouette of a person was barely visible as I remember it to this day – the patches of fog drifting slowly by the target with rain pelting the brim of my hat.

The ground was wet, and after about two hours, all my layers of clothing were soaked, and then water would drip off my cap into the rifle sight area. I thought if the enemy is out in this kind of weather at such a great distance, it is going to be very difficult to make a direct kill.

I was at an obvious handicap with the M-16 ejecting cartridges off my right cheek scorching my skin. The instructor advised I shoot from the right shoulder. I looked at him like he should go somewhere else and gave him the Indian silent treatment. Lefthanders are marksmen.

Somehow I scored an 86 on the rifle range, which were only a few points less than some of the better shooters.

I finished Basic Training in early March and bussed to Fort Leonard Wood, Missouri --to fulfill field wireman requirements and climbed some splintered wood poles.

On a humid morning at the pole training grounds, I was descending a thirty-foot pole when my gaff slipped and I came straight down with a robust four-inch splinter in my thigh. It didn't look near as bad as the fellow next to me who had a big hole in the toe of his boot.

I was taken to a hospital where a doctor pulled the splinter without anesthetic. I had heard the orderly say the supply was depleted.

The nurse had to hold me down, and finally I asked for a rag or something to put in my mouth as I was in much pain. She gave me one.

The next morning at the barracks, I woke up with a swollen red leg from top to bottom. There was still some splinter in there, so back I went to the hospital, where fortunately, there was a doctor there who had a straighter knife and some anesthesia.

I have a jagged scar in that area, but at least I was given compensation later on in life. And of course, my perpetrators would later take advantage and put an implant right in that area.

The injury was a blessing in disguise because it kept me back from graduating with my class and going to Vietnam.

I was sent to Ft. Riley, Kansas, where I would stay for the next twenty months with a class of draftees, and I made the best of it while I was there, befriending a guy named Craig, who was from Washington State.

We had some good times playing racquetball, going to concerts all over the mid-west, and lulling many evenings in the bars around Manhattan, Kansas. We hitchhiked nearly everywhere until I brought my car back from Norfolk one weekend. I doubt it was coincidental the programming sent my daughter there to college thirty years later when she still lived in Virginia. That was absurd.

The covert drug program I had avoided so long in my life started to surround me in the Army: drugs were everywhere in 1970 with soldiers bringing back hashish from Germany, heroin from Vietnam, and marijuana from Mexico. But I maintained my integrity and used very little.

My buddy's military term of service expired before mine, and when he left, I became rather depressed. We had done so much together. And now the Army ordered me to Korea,

I did not want to go and did everything I could to try and get reassigned to Stateside duty my last year. I visited Ft. Story near home trying to get a transfer but no one would be in the office when I got there.

Nothing worked, and in December of 1972 I found myself on an airplane after visiting a friend in Los Altos, leaving Travis Air Force Base in Oakland, California then stopping over in Japan for fuel and going to Korea.

When I arrived and bunked up for the night at Camp Casey, I got terribly sick. I don't know if it was from some partying I did with friends in Los Altos, California or from something I ate or drank after entering Korea. I vomited much and thought it was the end for me, one of the sickest moments of my life.

Somehow, I got on the back of a five-ton truck in the early morning hours at Camp Casey that was transporting a bunch of us to Camp Pelham near the Demilitarized Zone on a freezing night just before Christmas. I had ice on my pile cap from the ride. It was very cold.

The next day, I hired a houseboy to take care of making my bed, cleaning my clothes, and shining my shoes.

Settling into the bunk next to the potbelly diesel filled stove probably wasn't the best idea because it blew up on a chilly night and everyone had to go outside. Such was life in Korea.

Mornings were spent in the communication's shop trying to keep warm but occasionally we would venture out during the day and check out the wiring on the telephone poles. Eventually I would be assigned to change

41

it out with a group of mixed Republic of Korean and American soldiers.

It was a futile effort and I decided to look for another job. I'm not sure how I talked myself into getting the courier's job but it was the best thing that ever happened.

I now had my own jeep and would travel the country picking up and delivering classified information over the northern part of South Korea.

I suppose my perpetrators had me where they wanted me: having access to classified information. But I never had any intention of looking at what I was carrying. For one thing, items were sealed, and they didn't interest me. I was just glad to have a decent job away from the ROK soldiers who had excess kimchi on their breath and didn't want to take orders.

Off I would go every morning, stopping at several camps on the way to headquarters at Camp Casey. Then I would grab the latest edition of the Stars and Stripes newspaper, a cup of coffee, some doughnuts, and I'd lull around a couple hours at Camp Casey and head on back.

Just before arriving back at the compound, I'd drive the jeep through an ankle deep river to wash off the mud. The Army never complained about how it was done, but the Koreans downstream weren't too thrilled because I was disturbing the water and them washing clothes.

I didn't think they were sensitive about things in life considering they were hanging dogs and setting fire to them in preparation for dinner. But their cheesy looks usually told the story.

I would at this time thank a North Carolina native named Wallace who was a mechanic at the motor pool for gassing up my jeep: it was the fastest in the fleet.

Korea wasn't all bad. I met the most wonderful woman of my life there and I would stay with her every chance possible. We travelled to many places. We explored the country looking for ginseng, went to Seoul for

42

dining and lodging, and we went to Musan where there was a theatre.

It was hard to go wrong at that time when the train ride was eighty cents and the movie was twenty cents. I wish I could have brought her back, but I didn't have enough money for her plane fare.

After seven months in Korea, the Army offered me a promotion to Sergeant if I would enlist for six more years. I turned it down. I wanted to go home.

My perpetrators didn't like this and I was given extra duty picking up rocks out of ditches in the evening hours. Their excuse was that I talked back to an alcoholic Sergeant.

Why was it such a big deal that I did not re-enlist? But this is what targeted individuals go through when administrators of hate have access to manipulating events with their high-tech remote sensing applications.

In a normal world, no one would care, but in a targeted world, situations are manipulated around the victim for defamation, oppression, and servitude.

I would be confined to the Compound for two weeks, and I sure missed my girlfriend during those two weeks. I would look through the barbed wire fence across the creek to the village each night looking for her.

Staying at camp was miserable, so a friend Darren and I would go over to the club and began drinking mixed alcoholic drinks at 25 cents a pour until 2:00 in the morning and stagger back to the hooch -- only to hear the camp cannon fire one night three times -- twenty minutes later -- which means to get dressed for battle and attend a formation.

Man, I was sick, and I spent a considerable time throwing up my drinks on the side of the road as I was driving the First Lieutenant. That was a long day.

And then race relations deteriorated at the camp, which I do believe was programmed by the mass targeting

43

system. One night there was a big riot where lots of soldiers were getting hurt.

The officers thought the troops needed a twenty-five mile march to quiet them down -- and there we went with full battle gear up into the hills for an overnight march.

Some guys couldn't make it, and I begged for the medic to take my buddy back to camp in a vehicle after he told me his brother had died from such a march.

And they did take Darren back to camp. As a result, I was detailed to guard duty on the perimeter at 3: 00 a.m. I suppose for speaking up. A very lonely fox hole on a moonless night at the North Korea border.

I was determined to get out of Korea any way possible. A clerk at Camp Casey answered my prayers and asked me where I wanted to go.

"Home! Anywhere near home in Virginia."

"How about Fort Belvoir," he asked.

"That sounds good," I responded.

"But what's there?"

"A bricklaying class."

"Great."

On my next trip to Camp Casey, he had the orders signed for me -- an early two month exit from Korea. I was ecstatic.

Finally it came time for me to exit the country in October of 1973 and I had to travel from Camp Pelham to Camp Casey to catch the plane. It was about thirty miles south.

I thought I might stay with my girlfriend the night prior and leave from there early in the morning; however about 4:00 a.m., I heard the Camp cannon again fire three times—which meant to fall into group formation with full battle gear.

Now just how coincidental is that? It's not. It was just another attempt to try and delay me from leaving the country – for whatever reason. (Back home my mother's targeting would begin in earnest.)

There was no way I was going back to the Camp Pelham compound. I had my duffle bag packed with me. I hung out a few more hours with my girl, made more love, and said goodbye -- got a cab, and took the back roads to Camp Casey -- where I was immediately apprehended and taken to jail.

No problem. I knew all the officers at Camp Pelham from transporting them around all year and their secret documents. So, they wouldn't come get me, and in a couple of days I was on the plane heading to my next stop, Fort Belvoir. Bye. I heard later that my girlfriend went to the airport to check on me and waving as the plane flew off, and it just broke my heart, as I read her letter months later.

Project Transition was a program designed to give veterans job training to prepare them for civilian work upon leaving the Armed Forces. I was taking advantage of it.

I would hitch-hike home on weekends to see Mom and Kitty.

The perpetrators had been busy back in my hometown!

Mom had moved to an apartment near the beach, where she would be targeted heavily.

She loved the beach, probably trying to shut down her implants, and it would only be a two block walk to go swimming and sun bathing. If only she wouldn't have been targeted.

Mom's Targeting, 1974

My Army term of enlistment expired December 29, 1973, so I went to live with mom at her apartment on Kingston Avenue in Norfolk until I could find a place to live

I didn't have the faintest idea of what I was going to do for a living, and it took me some time to simply adjust to civilian life again though I'd been at Fort Belvoir for a couple of months.

The first couple of weeks found me going out with a friend to some old drinking spots and playing pool. And then we'd ride around and see some friends in the neighborhood. I'd stay over one friend's parent's house on weekends. This friend today is targeted heavily, with all kinds of electrical problems in his house, continual health problems, and hasn't worked since he was younger. I always wondered why he walked with his head and shoulders at an angle, and now I know. He was definitely implanted, which causes the muscles to tighten up in the body. And he always had the bed-wetting problems like most victims.

One of the dumbest things I did about this time was refusing to see my former girlfriend Kathy, who I had dated for years. I know now that was manipulated; the perpetrators would have their plan to set me up with another girl. And of course her last name would be synonymous with righteousness.

The perpetrators assign names to individuals and then get them to perform a name action. To give a broad example, a person who would be programmed to play tennis, would be named Loberly.

I see this all the time, and the public just doesn't understand what is happening.

Anyway, after a few weeks staying with mom and getting some unemployment pay, I started sharing an apartment with a guy from the old neighborhood. One night we double-dated some girls, and that's how I met Doris.

My roommate moved out shortly thereafter, and Doris, wanting to escape her mother's dominance, moved in. After all, I needed help with the rent.

Doris Johnson was a couple years younger than I. At the time, she was a sweet, bubbly, innocent girl that wanted big things in life. She admitted to not being the smartest woman; she barely passed high school.

I learned right off how little she knew about homemaking when she came into the living room one morning and asked me what I wanted for breakfast.

"Eggs and pancakes will be fine," I responded.

She walked back into the kitchen and I didn't hear anything for about ten minutes, wondering what she was doing.

Meekly she came back into the living room, "I don't know how to cook eggs."

So much for having a girlfriend that knew how to cook. So I taught her lots about cooking and gave her a good cookbook for Christmas.

I really don't think it was her that voluntarily changed for the worse, but these perpetrators changed her behavior somewhere along the way, emphatically nine years later when she went to New Jersey and represented Virginia in a beauty pageant sponsored by the *Big and Beautiful Women* organization. She came home a very different person, full of swelling pride and arrogance.

Anyway, Doris had got a job at a local grocery store paying union wages, so that was really good. We were in love, enjoyed our dates at the disco parlors at Virginia Beach, movies, and eating at the cafeterias.

47

I went to work for a Telephone Inter-connect company located in Chesapeake. The company installed PBX systems all over the Southeast United States and I would go as far west as Missouri where three of us technicians installed telephone systems in various motels.

Days Inn was a big client. But I tired of traveling. After all, I had just got out of the Army. The pay wasn't that great either at $3.00 per hour, but I did enjoy using the meal ticket.

I saved up some money and bought a 1957 Chevrolet, which used a lot of gas. Not a big deal back then, except the Arab oil embargo took place about this time.

Now that Doris and I had become situated, the devil would cause trouble.

Mother would come over to the apartment one morning paranoid as ever and wanted me to spend time with her.

She suspected someone was stalking her, had done something to the gas stove (which they had with the pilot light off and the smell of gas being emitted), and she couldn't sleep. Nothing could calm her down.

Upon questioning her, I found out she had been dating a 75 year old doctor from Maryland.

I have no doubt he was contracted to implant her with a remote sensing device. She was never the same after being with him, constantly humming some high pitched tune, nervous, paranoid, fidgety, and suspicious of everything.

So why was someone wanting to bother dear old mom? She wouldn't hurt no one or gossip about anything. At the time, she was working at Old Dominion University as a switchboard operator.

But this is what the stalker perpetrators do: they choose people who will be no threat to their evil activities.

Anyway, after trying to get mom to work off her anxiety by washing the car and doing some work around the house -- and seeing that nothing was working -- I called our family physician, Dr. Schechner, to get his advice.

"Put her in the psychiatric unit at DePaul Hospital," he said.

So mom and I talked it over, and she agreed to go to the Human Resources Institute – which is just what the perpetrators wanted.

Schechner, my childhood ear, nose, and throat doctor, may have been a player in this MK-Ultra program. From what I understand, many German doctors were used.

Mom did not like the Care Unit; she would not take medicine. She wanted out.

She did however stay about a month.

In the meantime, my brother came from Tennessee to visit her, and he made matters worse. Always a moocher, he used mom's car and wrecked it. I promptly told him to go back home.

After mom got out of the Care Unit, she still had the same problems: the implants can take years to finally dissipate and some never do.

But little was known about the life of implants in 1974 among the general public. I even had dad come over to the apartment one day to see if he couldn't calm her, but mom still acted fitfully.

In August of 1974, I called her brother Tom in Alabama to come and take her back to the Reservation.

Tom, a cabbie, made some money off the deal by selling mom's car and some household goods; then he took her to her sister's house in Montgomery, Alabama, where she stayed for awhile until she got a trailer on her land in Cherokee.

Mom lived in that trailer for a few years, but eventually got assistance from the Indians to build a house. (This is the same place where I would later find refuge after someone tried to kill me with direct energy in

49

a Virginia Beach apartment and a Norfolk Post Office mail room during a two week period in 1990 while appealing a divorce decree.)

After the episodes with mom, I was contemplating my life's future one morning sitting at the bottom of the stairwell on a concrete step at the parking area of the Hillside Avenue apartments where Doris and I lived.

The sun was shining between the tall apartment buildings at the parking lot entrance when out of nowhere a gust of wind made a whirlwind in the corner of the buildings and old trash and newspapers flew up into the air. Dust and debris twirling in a circle finally settled and one yellowed weathered page came across the concrete lot and rested at my feet.

Tentatively, I looked down at the weathered paper and an editorial page that stared at me -- where a letter I had written a month earlier to the editor had been published. Strange, or divine?

My perpetrators would not have wanted me to receive confidence from getting published in the paper; therefore, I would not have received this paper.

But God had other plans with that whirlwind and I kept this incident in the back of my mind for years. I always felt my spiritual gift was to write, but I've been shut down time and time again by unseen evil forces.

That's why I had to self-publish my devotional books, and I could find no help proof-reading or editing. The perpetrators went so far as to change words in *Devotions A-Z,* before it got printed. I corrected one word three times but it still got in the book as "do" rather than "to." And wouldn't you know they'd manipulate page sixty-six to make it look like I said we "are god" and not to be "with God."

Anyway, I was certainly honored to have a devotion printed by the Upper Room devotional magazine for Christmas Eve of 1999.

I quit the telephone interconnect company in 1974 and started working for the Holiday Inn downtown so I could be closer to home and Doris, who was definitely careless with money, time, and commitment. I learned later she was seeing an old boyfriend.

Poor girl just couldn't control her life. But I understand what was controlling her: she had no idea.

I found myself having to protect her more than equally sharing our lives. After all, she made a big mistake one night hitch-hiking from the beach with her girlfriend and finding herself in a man's strange apartment being forced to do unnatural things. She was mindless at times. Maybe that's because she admitted to breathing in exhaust smoke from the school bus because it smelled good.

At one point, she got very sick from not taking care of herself and ended up in the hospital being diagnosed with hepatitis. Girl looked awful, with yellow colored eyes and pale skin. She wouldn't eat right and now she was paying the price. Her cigarette smoking and continual drinking of Tabs didn't help much.

I got a job at the Holiday Inn downtown. Being a doorman was a menial job but I had a lot of fun. Many a celebrity would stay at the Inn, because it was next door to Chrysler Hall and the Scope Arena in downtown Norfolk. I would get to chauffeur the likes of Paul Lynde, Tony Randall, Pearl Bailey, and others. I made money by tips and wages, put food on the table, and settled into a homely life with Doris, who was learning to cook, sew, and all the other things a woman is supposed to know. We were a happy but young couple with a just a few responsibilities.

I do believe I was manipulated to run Mayor Jordan's handicapped drivable car through the glass doors one night at the Inn. I couldn't get the gas pedal to release itself.

51

Anyway, when the rental lease expired at the apartment, I tried to separate from Doris and get my own apartment. I wanted to get closer to Old Dominion University where I could attend classes with my G.I. Bill and learn something that would get me a good job. But as I was leaving the apartment and looked back at the top steps, Doris was sitting there crying heavily. She did not want to go back to her mother.

I told her to come on and we moved into a cute little duplex, but it was near the Naval Air Base where a lot of sailors could be unruly at times. One day a local sailor would find his way to the back door of the apartment and try to enter. Doris, having been abused once in her life, chased him off with a knife.

We were going to have to move.

A Programmed Marriage

Doris and I got married June 29, 1975.

It was a beautiful ceremony at the Botanical Gardens at Norfolk International Airport with azaleas blooming and turtles sunning on rocks in the nearby ponds.

People thought we were getting married because she was pregnant, but that was not true. So we spent that first year happy to be on our own in a nice little duplex apartment with me working at the hotel and Doris down the street at Big Star stores.

Then I got a job with the Postal Service and went to work on my birthday of May 22, 1976.

Doris got pregnant a few months later, and after some guy tried to get in the apartment and assault Doris, I decided it was best for us to go out and get a house, for Doris's safety and for the baby.

But it was a bad decision to get this house though it was a beautiful brick home.

There was a detective who lived caddy corner, a tugboat operator in back of us, and a flooring installer across the street. They were all pretty normal people. But it was a corner house in a strategic location across from some apartments on the Virginia Beach side of the road.

I should have known there was a bad omen at the house when the couple who had lived there were getting a divorce; they were just as fine a couple as you would want to meet. Now I know that such house numbers as 6156 are merely tags for the targeting.

About this time, Dad and I start renewing our relationship, playing cribbage on the weekends, and socializing. He was excited about his forthcoming grandchild.

Sarah was born at 6: 12 p.m., on June 9, 1977. (That's right 6:12 on 6/9.) I'm sure the perpetrators orchestrated the timing as much as I did to delay it. The doctor insisted on using forceps around three o'clock in the afternoon.

But I adamantly told him no.

No one was forcing my child's birth: I would wait on the Lord. As it was, she had a bit of a bruise on her head that I wondered about, but it was probably from the delivery itself.

Doris and I and Sarah enjoyed our first few years later at the house.

I was working the night shift at the Post Office mail processing center, but it allowed me time to watch Sarah during the day, up until the time Doris got home from her part-time job at a bakery.

I'd dress Sarah up, fix her hair, and we'd take off on the bicycle to the library about three miles away with a stop at McDonalds. On Friday nights, we'd end up at the mall in one of the bookstores, with her finding a comfortable spot reading and I'd be checking out everything from bicycle touring to health remedies.

Doris's mother was of little help; she had health problems that prevented her from babysitting.

Around 1978, Dad was diagnosed with cancer, and I'm sure this sickness was manipulated.

But Dad did smoke a lot of cigarettes and drank a lot of coffee. That would just give the perpetrators however a reason to make cancer with their black neurotoxins.

That's what they look for. I've had numerous natural injuries way before the perpetrators decided to inject their evil implants into me; such as a burn mark I had received as a child when I got too close to a hot iron; and the shoulder burn area on my shoulder from carrying a golf bag.

Both places would be implanted.

I also have an implant in hernia repair scar tissue --
that at one time was just as smooth as my regular skin.

Thirty years later, at a time when I was encouraging
my disabled second wife to wash good around her belly
button, an implant would be covertly placed on me in the
same area. There was no bump under the skin until that
time.

There are objects just below the skin all over my body!

Upon applying a rare earth magnet, which I assume
increases the electron activity of the implant and causes it
to expand, in most cases, a black polymer carbonized
looking substance will surface.

My neck, throat, arms, and legs all have implants
that were covertly placed, usually near specific nerve
functions.

Sometimes these substances will exit the needle
perforations – unless they have coagulated in the blood
and find a joint area – such as the active wrists --- to build
up and finally exit.

Anyway, Dad went into the hospital for awhile, and
about the same time, my brother encouraged me to
confront him about our dysfunctional upbringing.

I really had no intention to confront my sick father in
the hospital.

But I did one afternoon, after I stopped and got a
beer at a downtown bar, and it was one of the worst
things I have ever done in my life .It wasn't dad's fault we
were all targeted.

James blamed Dad for the bad things that had
happened to him: taking him off the high school baseball
team because of bad school grades -- and other things. My
brother could not let go of the hatred he had. This
attitude was definitely attributable to the targeting that
most victims talk about dividing families.

I went to the hospital and told Dad about how James
and I had been cheated out of childhood because he wasn't

there. I carried on for about fifteen minutes and then left the room.

This is what the perpetrators and manipulation system does – defames and demoralizes a person even when they are already at their lowest. And I was used by the system.

About six months later, Dad entered a long-term care hospital. I visited him occasionally. He continued to get worse. I still had some anger in me about my upbringing, but one night, at my mother's insistence, I would go and visit and ask for forgiveness for my behavior.

I put my head on his frail chest and asked him to forgive me.

I'll never forget his words.

"Forgiveness should be an everyday part of our lives, shouldn't it?" he said.

That was the graciousness and kindness of my dad.

And he forgave me. My brother was not so fortunate, even though I had warned him the previous week about Dad's pending death, James would not come.

A few hours after I had left the hospital and went home, I got a call from the hospital saying my father had passed away.

I was astounded that God cared enough for me to redeem me of sin at a last critical moment.

I went to the hospital, confirmed the death, made sure his time-piece was on his wrist as requested, and went straight to a beach area where I could pray.

I could tell someone was remotely monitoring me, and I don't think it was ironic I ended up mourning at the same place where dad often fished for speckled trout at Lynn-haven Inlet. Like father, like son, is the perpetrators motto.

Lynn-haven Inlet was full of intelligence agency activities; it being the first inlet from the entrance to the Chesapeake Bay where ships from the Navy travelled the

Atlantic Ocean, and foreign ships daily navigated the channel to dock at the International Port terminal.

I continued in prayer beside the rushing tidal water over a moonlit river channel. Warily I looked up at the sign posted on the vehicle bridge concrete piling that listed the amount of people who had drowned in the swift moving water in the inlet.

Dad spent many days there fishing, as he used to live in a single bedroom apartment just down the road shortly after he and mom were divorced. I'd been there several times and was treated to a porterhouse steak and baked potato, and then we'd play cribbage and watch a game on television.

I felt a lot closer to him beside the waters but I could definitely feel an abnormal light hitting me. I looked around to see nothing but the parking lot with one occupied car.

My mother and brother would not come to the funeral; neither of them were mentally stable enough to make the trip for one thing.

I was so thankful to the American Legion assembly that hosted the funeral. They didn't have to come, but because I was an Army veteran, and they cared, they came.

But after Dad's death, I felt lost – and stressed from mainly being on my job as a letter sorting machine clerk.

On the weekends, I would go fishing with my friend Russell, and we would enter some of the local foot races. But God had other plans for me.

My physical health began to deteriorate, and one night, I passed out on the workroom floor while standing casing magazines.

Tired from being on the machine, breathing in the dust at the Post Office, not being with the family at nights, and my health failing, something had to give.

I thought maybe I was just having food allergies, but shots made it worse.

Deep in my spirit, I knew there were problems. Doris and I were spending hardly any time together, the mortgage had to be paid, I had a child, and I was feeling very insecure.

A New Journey, 1981

After the time of the leg injury and my spiritual conversion in the beginning of this book, I continued to walk more and more each day. I would take Sarah with me and we would walk up to six miles! God bless her.

But by then I was financially hurting from being out of work at the Post Office.

My sick leave has been used up. My wife was working only part-time, and I had a mortgage with a four year old child.

But relief came when the Post Office brought me back to work as a part-time Postage Due clerk for four hours a day, and I was able to sit down performing the work.

Walking by the letter sorting machine brought back terrible memories. I would be no longer able to beg my way off because I was getting physically better. But I could neither stand for long periods of time at a distribution case sorting mail.

What was I going to do?

The underlying factor behind all these injuries was a result of my MK-Ultra targeting. These accidents were all tests and acts of sadism -- targeting designed to put me down and be disabled.

When I look back on the timing, I was hurt right before I had five years total in the Post Office, which would have excluded me from receiving disability benefits.

But I had enough sick leave to surpass the five year mark.

I might add also about the time of the leg injury, a bump would appear at the top of that femoral nerve on the left thigh. Now I sense that was a microchip. Years later, I would find another of the black particles at the bottom of the left calf muscle and foot.

It's no different when the covert perpetrators put a microchip in my right shoulder around 1999, along with what looked like a microscopic antenna about 7/16" long.

I made a vow to get off the green monster. I would be no longer able to beg my way off once I got physically better. And I could no longer stand for long periods of time at distribution cases sorting mail. I really didn't know what the future held. I had tried for years to get a transfer to a smaller town, but Doris would have none of it. And the Postal Service just wouldn't move me.

I had to think about getting another job; so I started taking typing classes at the local college before work. A couple of months went by. My leg and faith were getting stronger.

After sitting in the Postage Due Clerk's seat boringly marking up mail for correct postage, I was asked to fill in for the Training Technician's job upstairs during lunch hour.

I had been an expert operator, so maybe that's why management figured I'd be a good substitute trainer. But more than likely, it was because I was restricted to sitting down until my leg healed.

Employees would come in each hour to receive training on new address changes or learn a particular group of zip codes and the associated carrier information. New-hires would come in for pre-employment screening to see if they were fit to key on the monster. If they failed the test, they went back home.

But this job was a test for me also.

The targeting had isolated me in my own thoughts for years, and now I had to interact with a lot of different personalities.

For those of you who don't understand the targeting process, it is a constant barrage of non-ionizing

60

frequencies hitting the head, with magnetic fields to manipulate and influence thoughts and moods.

And the targeting can also influence people around you to be paranoid or whatever.

In my teen years, the program would send repeating sounds of music at me. Many God-fearing church people think because they are humming a song after the church service, it's because they like the song.

Wrong. They are being sent a repetitive man-made signal that many victims say is intentional and coming from microwave repeaters.

I'm not a sound technician, but I can assure you the patents are registered for the technology.

After a couple of months passed, a permanent training technician's job opened, and fortunately for me, I was able to qualify for the typing requirement because I had been practicing at a local college.

But it certainly wasn't easy, having to type 45 words per minute for five minutes with less than two errors.

Anyway, I applied for the job and won out over a union steward by one point. The job selection was contested but I prevailed.

This was great for me because I now had a sit down job and my leg could continue to heal.

About a year later, Norfolk was scheduled to be the main location for mechanized mail distribution for the entire Hampton Roads area, so many associate distribution offices would have to make the transition.

Manual clerks from the surrounding six cities would need to be trained on the letter sorting machine. Many clerks balked at the new change but wanted the higher pay, the union agreement mandated compliance.

I would be training clerks on the night shift. I mainly conducted orientation classes and initial scheme training on carrier routes. Some nights as many as one hundred people would come into the training room, which does not please the average training instructor. No more than ten per hour gives a training technician time to help each person and answer questions. But the mechanization process would proceed, because man-hours must be saved, and the Post Office was in deep financial debt.

The stresses of this job were tremendous, but I had always got along good with people and this job would prove no different. I was well liked and fair to everyone when administering tests and scores.

And then I began to set my sights on a Postmaster job in a small town anywhere. But the program wouldn't allow it. So I was stuck.

During the time as a trainer, I was able to suggest new mail processing routings which resulted in several monetary awards.

But I was still suffering: my leg was gaining strength but my weight went down to 157 pounds, and I was 6'0 tall.

After four years in this position, I honestly couldn't take no more. The chain driven machine noise in the enclosed room was awful. One of those years was spent on the graveyard shift and the others during the evening hours. But it did allow me watch and spend time with Sarah.

Doris was not much for help: she seemed bent on escaping home life and going places, and this is just about the time she represented Virginia in the *Big and Beautiful Women* pageant in New Jersey. She had won several local beauty contests around the area, and she met the weight and height requirements for the contest; so off she went with a sponsor or two that furnished the clothing.

I wished her well.

Fortunately for me, I had friends at work, and when I had a hernia operation around 1982, Rosalynn would be there for me.

She'd often eat lunch with me in the training area and we'd talk about religion, jobs, and people. She was a former airline pilot who was dismissed from her job for some reason. Anyway, Rosalynn enabled me to see how sad my life had become. I was in a dead end trainer's job stuck behind stressful, dark, walls, and the Post Office was not going to promote me, even after all the courses I had taken to be a small town postmaster. My boss Corrine, sensed the problems I had at home, and she wasn't going to move me. Rosalynn and her husband eventually moved and I never saw them again.

A change had to take place, and I started applying for other jobs. I had fulfilled my duties in this job for the past five years and got the mechanization program off to a great start, having qualified at least 200 operators, so it was time to go.

I applied for an Intelligence Clerk's job at the Naval Base, which was probably a programmed application. Thankfully, I got turned down for the job.

My perpetrators were trying to fulfill their mission to have me become a spy. Spy books had consumed most of my book reading as a kid. Hiding behind trees and bushes watching cars and people go by on the major roads occupied many late afternoons. And I had been a courier for classified information in South Korea in the Army. And now they had a plan to get me in such a job, divorce my wife and family so I would be alone.

I even went to the Air Force Reserve office one day and signed up to be a cartographer -- filled out all the papers -- but at the last minute I changed my mind and threw everything away.

At this point of 32 years in my life, I had turned to God for guidance.

In the meantime, I still needed my job, and suddenly the one I had was being reverted: the duties were being changed and the job would be posted for bidding.

I was told not to worry about it but to simply reapply. I was the most qualified obviously for my own job anyway.

But right about the time I got a comforting call from my boss about the job, some strange external energy came over me. I went outside for a walk to try and figure out what was happening. I was very much in touch with my body and I knew this was nothing within me. This was being conducted remotely. It was the first time I had ever been aware of such adverse energy, and it was not a coincidence it was taking place.

I saved my job and continued to work another year in the training room, but I was still tiring of the position; so I continued filling out applications for other jobs, and when a Procurement Clerk's job opened, I applied and got it.

It was a thankless job, taking care of the Postal Library and inventory of supplies. I packaged and shipped supplies daily to Stations and Branches in the Virginian Eastern District. And I had an added duty – to go up to the mail room at the end of each day to duplicate memorandums and policies and disseminate them to all the Stations and Branches. But I was basically my own boss.

I was growing stronger in my spiritual relationship with God, but being a Procurement Clerk did not fulfill God's plan; there was still this targeting stuff going on.

Every time I walked by the Box Section in the Mail Processing area I got terribly dizzy. A couple of times I had to lay down for a short time in the locker room, it was so bad. I still don't know if that was incidental or purposed, but it was real.

Of course now I know, but in 1986 I didn't know a third party was out to destroy my life.

About this time In February of 1986, something strange happened that confirmed I was targeted. On an otherwise dreary quiet Saturday afternoon, I received a phone call from a man with a very deep voice asking me to come to the beach and identify a ring with my initials – he wanted to give me money for it.

I hadn't the faintest idea of who this could be since I was hardly socializing off-hours with anyone, and at the time, I couldn't think of any ring I had possibly lost. I had stopped wearing jewelry for years since I had been working around postal machinery.

I declined the offer of meeting at the beach to get the expensive ring, for it sounded like a set-up or something. Years later I kept thinking about that call, and then I finally remembered I had lost a nice tiger eye stone set in gold sometime after I got out of the Army. Had these people been cataloging my every possession since 1974 and stealing my goods to try and blackmail me? I think so. I've had things show up in my trailer where someone had held onto them for nearly five years! The perpetrators had actually transported goods from North Carolina to South Carolina and put them in my trailer! Some of the goods had been gone up to seven years! But when they're killing scheme didn't work, they returned lots of stuff.

Wanting to find some peace in my life and good health, I started praying about where the Lord would want me. Sarah was now old enough where she needed to go to school in a stable community -- unlike Norfolk which is a highly transient place.

And I wanted freedom from the rat race.

And there was only one such place in my mind: Western North Carolina.

Mother and I had visited Cherokee many times throughout my youth, and I envisioned again walking by the clear streams, climbing the mountains, and sitting by the wood stove on cold winter nights eating home made sauerkraut, corn pones, and fried ramp onions.

I had had enough of punching the clock and working in a job at all kinds of hours and not seeing my family or enjoying life.

Feelings of the peace in Cherokee and surrounding mountains had stayed with me through the Army, marriage, and my job. Sometime, I would be going there for good.

I would quit the Post Office, take my little bit of retirement, buy a book store, and live happily ever after.

I talked Doris into this idea somewhat, and she wanted to host a delicatessen there of some sort.

In March 1986, we put the house up for sale and took off to North Carolina to seek out my dream. Doris and Sarah would come back by bus, so Sarah could finish school, and by that time the house should be sold.

But things would end up much different, my downfall beginning in earnest.

March 1986

For affliction does not come forth from the dust, nor does trouble spring up out of the ground; for man is born to trouble, and the sons of the flame rise, flying upward.

Job 5: 7

Doris, Sarah, and I took off to mom's house and stayed for a night; then they went back on a bus to take care of selling the house in Norfolk while Sarah was finishing up school.

In the back of my mind, I wondered about my marriage. Doris did not want to move away from her mother, and she had filed for divorce five years earlier but nothing came of it.

I had never forgotten about it.

But she had no reason to divorce now: I was going to church and humbled myself to all her desires. And I spent every available moment with Sarah.

But I really didn't know Doris any longer. Much of my time was spent at the Post Office, and she was spending time with her friends at the theatre.

I was glad she was having fun, but I hoped it wouldn't be at mine and Sarah's expense.

I enjoyed being at mom's house. I volunteered at the local library for awhile, walked the trails, and got to know the local folk. I liked it so much I decided to quit the Post Office back in Norfolk and sent them a letter of resignation. I felt stress-free for the first time in ten years.

But the remote targeting would cause chaos.

Mother would turn against me, and back home, Doris would be talking to friends about getting a divorce.

Nearly all victims of electronic harassment report this same targeting scenario: a mood of distrust is sent among the family members to try and isolate the targeted individual.

Some victims feel this is a program to make lonely people some kind of sex slaves, and much of the targeting stimulates sexual desires when the electromagnetic fields are manipulated to force the blood down to the genitals.

I had heard about this happening to victims over the conference calls, and then it started happening to me. Fortunately, I was able to recognize it.

There was really no reason to become passionate at certain times of the day, and victims had also found implants in their private areas.

Mom wanted me out a week or so before I was planning on leaving.

But I was hardly ready to leave the area because I was waiting for responses to a couple job applications. I wanted to stay in North Carolina for awhile longer, but mom made it unbearable, so I turned to my aunt for help: she lived next door.

Aunt Betsy said I could stay in her shed, which was fine with me because it was warm enough and I would be away from dissension and could still go to her house to eat.

But after I ate some baked chicken one day, I got terribly sick. Betsy had left some oven cleaner in her oven that had dried up, and I had baked the chicken with it in there.

I got very ill, and then she wanted me out.

Did the perpetrators manipulate this scheme? These are the kind of events they manipulate using mood alteration and electronic targeting by computer programs.

God bless her though; she had mercy enough to get me an apartment down the road and I stayed there for a week or so until I called Doris one night.

I told her I had blood poisoning and would have to delay my return.

Doris responded over the phone, "You stay there."

And she hung up.

Sensing something very wrong, I called my real estate agent, and I found out Doris had taken the house off the market.

A Programmed Divorce 6/12/86

Why is light given to the miserable one? And life to him who is bitter in soul; who is waiting for death, and it is not; and they dig for it more than for treasures? They are rejoicing to exultation. They are glad when they find the grave. To a man whose way is hidden, God has made a hedge about him. For my sighing comes before my food; and my groanings are poured out before the waters. For the dreadful thing I dreaded has come upon me; and that which I feared has come to me. I am not at ease, nor at rest; nor am I quiet, yet trouble comes.

Job 3: 20-26

I immediately packed my bags and headed off to Norfolk while my stomach churned with anxiety and panic thoughts invaded my mind, mostly because of the poison I had ingested, and my electronic targeting.

Before I went over the mountain leaving the Reservation, I stopped off at a favorite spring to get what I knew would be one last drink of fresh spring water in the Appalachians.

The water did me no good. I was still light-headed, anxious, and poisoned.

I drove all night, and arrived home around 7:00 a.m. on the morning of June 13.

I knocked on the door and Doris opened it looking dazed and confused.

I kissed her on the cheek, and said, "Hi. Can you watch Sarah while I get a few hours sleep?"

There was no response from her; so nothing had changed.

She went and got Sarah and they left.

I went into the bedroom and saw my clothes had been packed.

How nice of her I thought, to get all my goods and pack them for our trip back to North Carolina.

The thought never entered my mind that she was going to ship my goods to me.

Doris called later in the day and said there was a separation agreement on the table—and that I'd better sign it.

I ignored her suggestion and went about my business trying to get my stomach calmed. There was a clumpy feeling in the bottom of my esophagus and I felt dizzy with nausea. Finally I gathered enough nerve to look over the papers and saw that she wanted a divorce, Sarah, the house, alimony, child support, and my retirement!

Doris was to be staying over her mother's house.

I went over there a couple of days later to try and find out what was happening with her, but her mother said Doris was bound and determined to get a divorce.

I called her later and told her that if she went through with the divorce – the lawyers would get a lot of money and probably the house.

There was still no response.

I looked up some of my childhood friends for support, and my old buddy Briley came over and spent some time with me, so that helped a lot.

Three weeks later, her lawyer filed a bill of complaint that stated I had deserted my wife, had no intention to come home, failed to support her and said I had come home and physically forced her out of our house.

Every statement was a lie, and this was from a man who represented a Norfolk district in the House of Delegates.

I visited my pastor for some prayer, and it had turned out, Doris had seen him also.

"She came to see me not long ago," he said.

"And what did she want?"

71

"She wanted a divorce."

"And what did you say?"

"I told her I would not encourage it but God wants us to be at peace."

In other words, he gave her spiritual permission to leave!

This is after he prayed for us for years to have a strong marriage.

But anyway, I still hoped God would bring her home.

Ill-advised, I took the pastor's suggestion and hired a Protestant pastor who said he handled domestic affairs.

But when I went to his office, he said he didn't want to get involved into the complexities of the case.

I needed someone to get involved!

He did make a court appearance for me, but Doris' attorney threatened the judge with a non-reappointment to the bench -- that caused him to rule in his favor and have me removed from my house! Talk about corruption and undue influence!

Plus, I would have to pay $550.00 a month which he divided up between alimony and child support.

I fired Williams, and, re-evaluating my predicament, which went against pastor's wishes to do nothing and suffer blame, started looking for another attorney.

I knew Doris was being influenced by her lawyer, but I had to protect myself legally.

Upon a recommendation from the real estate agent (Cas-on), I hired a well know lawyer in downtown Norfolk, who was a partner with three other attorneys.

He sounded strong and confident over the phone. "Come in tomorrow about 1:00 and bring a $1,000 retainer fee."

I arrived at his high rise office in downtown Norfolk around 1:00 in the afternoon but still in my sickened state.

"Tell me what happened," he said.

So I told him the story about Doris and me agreeing to go to North Carolina and looking for another place to live and work: she would come back and sell the house and join me after Sarah finished school.

"Well, what did she do when you came back?"

"I kissed her on the cheek and she took off somewhere with Sarah and never came back," I exclaimed for the third time.

"She left you!"

"Yeah, that's right. She left me!"

Mr. Fortner made an attempt to keep me in the house but the Judge wouldn't consider reversing his original order — after the legislator had threatened his re-appointment.

Fortner asked the court to keep the separation intact and sell the house at a later date, which I had agreed to beforehand.

So I was basically evicted from my home because of Doris and her attorney lying about me coming home and forcing her out.

Thinking this was all a bad dream or something, and there was a possibly of a chance of Doris dismissing the lawsuit, I got a room with weekly rates at a motel, just a couple miles from where Dad had lived in the apartment at Lynn-haven Inlet and where I had sat on the beach after his death.

The perpetrators program events such as these and they consider a son or daughter to follow in the parents footsteps.

As sick as I was at this time, I was under the perpetrators influence.

The motel at least offered me some seclusion and a chance to get well.

But it was at least a couple of weeks or so before I got better, spending evenings with inflamed lungs, congestion, and anxiety.

After I got back to the room one Sunday afternoon from a walk and prayer, I went across the street to the fish market, got some mackerel, red pepper, and lemon juice.

And the prayer of faith shall save the sick, and the Lord shall raise him up; and if he have committed sins, they shall be forgiven him.
                                                            James 5: 15-16

I ate this for two days and finally felt the pain around my chest leave. The infection was gone, and my senses returned. It was like I had awakened from a bad dream, but by now, I was losing my house, money, and family.

I felt a surge of strength but I was definitely angry someone would try and take advantage of me when I was sick. So I would attempt to reclaim all that was mine.

Shortly after I got better, I challenged a guest sailor to a game of chess and beat him both times.

So I knew I was ready to fight back, but a big hole was dug for sure. I had a wife who was being deceived and programmed, and I was now being stalked.

Loud parties started taking place in the room next door at the motel, and I knew it was purposed and time to leave.

Meanwhile, I took a job with Roadway Package Service as a delivery man for a couple of weeks.

But seeing the need to make more money, because of alimony and the child support payment, I called the Post Office.

It was an embarrassing phone call after I had quit a few months earlier, but it was my only choice to get some funds to pay the lawyer and the temporary support.

I was scheduled for an interview, at which time I stated I would rather have a carrier job this time. They obliged, but first they put me on a collections route part-time at night, picking up mail from downtown mailboxes.

To me, this was wonderful -- freedom from the work I had done previously at the Post Office sitting at desks and machine consoles for nine years. It didn't matter what hours they have to pick up mail.

After two months on the collection route, they let me deliver mail but first they tested me to see if my leg could withstand the stress of walking up steps. They had me deliver an hour's worth of mail in an older section of Norfolk that had houses with lots of steps.

Was it a coincidence Mr. Fortner's house just happened to be on that delivery route that day?

But getting a job back with the Post Office as a letter carrier increased my morale tremendously.

Once I got stationed at the Norfolk downtown Post Office, I moved from the motel closer to downtown Norfolk so the travel time would be less.

A friend, John, had told me there was an apartment available just below him. After contacting the owner, Mr. Gagne, and giving a deposit, I moved in.

I found it strange one day when I went out looking for a newspaper to read on Sunday morning and went to the Holiday Inn downtown. As I exited the drive from a downhill ramp, Fortner's car was coming from the opposite way, and I suppose he was heading to his office on the other side of town to do some work. He saw me looking at him and swerved as if he thought I was going to hit him. I was just sitting there waiting for traffic to pass, but his guilty conscience got the best of him I suppose. He was sending outrageous bills.

The harassment didn't quit. When I got to the new apartment in Norfolk, my tires would be flattened before an important court date. Thank God I had two cars in my possession, and then my friend who had helped me find the apartment, suddenly had a heart attack at thirty some years old!

After spending a couple of months filling in for other carriers and delivering their routes (after all, I knew about every route from the training room), I eventually got my own route. And then the harassment really picked up.

One day while I was delivering mail at Gray's Pharmacy, four ugly men stared at me as I passed their table: I had never seen them before in my life.

And the clerk at the register would propose a date, saying she wanted to learn about the Post Office. I almost fell for it and agreed to meet her at her apartment but I cancelled at the last hour. The winking of her eye had given her intent away.

Walking out of the pharmacy that day, a man would pass by the delivery truck and yell out, "You don't understand, do you?"

I continued on my way to deliver the mail to the Seven-Eleven store.

A few blocks later, after I had distributed mail in the foyer of an apartment complex, the four men blocked the exit at the main entrance, so I exited using another door, and at the nearest pay phone, called my pastor for some support.

He told me to use to super-natural prayer or something like that.

The delivery route I had at this time was located adjacent to Old Dominion University.

One of the lawyer partners in the firm lived on this route. I suppose this too was a coincidence. But I thought it strange when I was awarded a route closer to my original home years later and yet another of the firm's attorney's lived on that route. So what was that all about?

And the perpetrators would set up false businesses to try and get me in trouble.

One incident I had was near the Ingleside section, a route I had for about a year. It was murderous because it was about five miles walking.

I became suspicious shortly after I got the route when a sign business suddenly entered a vacant building.

This business got a lot of mail from lawyers I noticed! I mean, one day I delivered about 15 letters from different legal firms that were located in the Norfolk area! So this business was obviously some kind of clearing house for something.

As I made my way up to the steps to the office one day, I wondered about this place. There was a man behind the desk in the office. He had his arm in a sling, which was probably a fake injury, because shortly after I handed him the mail to his good hand, he asked me to open the envelope.

This was a big frame job. I declined, knowing it was against the law to open anyone's mail. I reported this incident to my supervisor the next day.

Doris' attorney saw that I had become stable and that I wanted my day in court, so he started finding excuses to go to Richmond and delay trial.

Interrogatories took place, because I was certainly interested in knowing what Doris was thinking about when she filed this suit.

As a result of her answers, she would be caught in a lie a year later at a commissioner's hearing.

But I'll never forget what her attorney said at a hearing, "I haven't attacked his health."

Never threaten anyone with an attack on health. I made my prayer to God right then about the statement.

Fortner made a similar comment over the phone one day, saying he had not put pressure on me. This is after I had been stalked, been sent frivolous legal bills, and scorned at a hearing for just sitting there when my wife threw a tantrum in the hallway.

And one day, as I waiting to come into his office, one of his partners entered my waiting area and told me to get out!

I had never seen the man in my life, but I can assure you I never forgot about his bad manners; an appeal from the eventual decree with the firm's name on it would take care of that.

Comical however, was seeing Doris one day in court kick her attorney in the knee with him throwing his clipboard across the room.

Fortner and I just looked at each other in disbelief and shook our heads. I had had enough of the scene and told them I was already late on my route and had several hundred welfare checks to deliver. Doris' attorney looked at me crazily, and I could sense he thought he was the only one in Virginia who gave poor people assistance in his Delegate duties.

During this time, there must have been five judges involved in my case. I had heard the term "judge shopping," and now I saw it.

Pastor and I prayed for Doris to come to know Jesus in her heart. But the worldly system and the lawyers made it easier for her to walk away.

Some one year after the filing is when the commissioner's hearing took place.

Doris' lawyer would ask why I wasn't with my child on a certain weekend. Fortunately, I had kept a letter that Doris had written showing he had advised her to keep Sarah.

So I told him, "Because you told Doris to take her away."

"Can you prove that?" he asked.

Reaching with my hand towards the file and looking at him, I said, "Yes."

Fortner slowly moved the file towards me opening it to the letter, bless his soul, and I proceeded to read where he advised Doris to take Sarah.

Embarrassed, especially in front of the Commissioner, he said he had no more questions.

Doris got terribly upset and walked out of the room twice with her words echoing throughout the room: "I thought it was a good time to take advantage of him. I knew he was sick, and I didn't think he could make it."

That was not the woman I had married who was speaking.

Such testimony was proffered to the original response and offered to the court, but I could tell my attorney was anxious about it on the way out of the building..

I yelled out, "Don't worry, the good Lord is with us."

He said, "But we got to be with Him."

I said, "I am with Him."

Generational Programming

I would find Sarah crying incessantly one Saturday afternoon when I called her on the phone, and I found the situation not much different from twenty-five years earlier when I woke up screaming with an earache, just like when my mother was in Richmond getting married, which is just where Doris was with her boyfriend this Saturday.

It was then I began to figure out the programming, the sordid character of it, and the sadistic nature of using children.

I went to the house to console her, but she now felt distrustful of me, but that's what the targeting is designed to do.

Looking into the bedroom revealed a man's robe on the bed post, and I became infuriated. So I went out to the car, got my camera, and came back into the house to take pictures and immediately sent them to Fortner.

I also remember playing across the street from my house in Fox Hall and my father driving up in his Monaco Dodge. He got out of the car and went and knocked on the door of our house in Fox Hall, for which he had been gone from some time.

Rather than go greet him, I froze behind the neighbor's azalea bush, just as the programming was designed to do.

My father had never hurt me, nor was he a violent man. So there was really no reason for me to not go and greet him, unless I was being manipulated. And I was being manipulated, because it was about this time in life, I started hearing resonating sounds around my head! (Pulsed microwave radiation.)

Anyway, I wanted the stranger and his clothing out of my house, and I got an order from the court to keep him out.

But I could not undo what had probably happened to Sarah that Friday night. Just as I when my mother went to Richmond; they probably got to her.

The results of the commissioner's hearing came fifteen months after the bill of complaint had been filed: Doris had deserted me. Now I was ordered to just pay child support.

Fortner would hold onto this divorce opinion and take off to Europe – to spend my money I suppose.

Persecution

Jesus said there would be persecutions, and now I believed it! Men were following me, noise was penetrating my apartment, and now a car mechanic tells me all but two loose lug nuts are missing from the left wheels of my car. Someone wants me dead, but who?

Could it be my lawyer trying to murder me? To make sure he would not get disciplined by the State Bar for failing to file appropriate objections in the trial court to protect my retirement?

Could it be my wife's attorney, who is a State legislator and would be highly embarrassed because he had filed a frivolous lawsuit against me?

And wasn't he the one driving around in back of my work area at the Post Office one day spying on me as I got off work? The only reason I had seen him is because I was looking out a fourth floor window of the Janaf Office building where my new girlfriend worked.

There he was, in his fancy maroon colored car sitting in an area behind the Post Office.

Or could it be my wife, who stands to lose our house she is living in because I am forcing the court to sell it? And it was her boyfriend I saw walking up and down the street below my apartment last Sunday morning.

These are the questions that plagued my mind on a hot day in the summer of 1988 as I looked at the lug-less studs on the two left wheels of my vehicle.

But shortly, I will be free from this mess, I think. *The divorce will be final, the house will be sold, and I will exit peacefully from this God abandoned city and into my native country.* Or so I thought.

Justice

Several months after the commissioner's hearing, I still didn't have my divorce decree, and I couldn't get any response from my attorney.

I had no choice but to file suit: I wanted to go on with my life.

I mean, there was absolutely nothing else left to do, other than partition the house.

One of his interns showed up at court, and we came to an agreement to get my divorce decree in ten days.

On Sept 16, 1988, the two attorneys argued behind closed doors.

I found out about the closed door hearing from the court clerk, so I immediately went to get a copy.

Monday I got the decree, and my anxiety was definitely relieved.

She would not receive alimony or the house she had planned to get in the beginning.

Now I would only have to go through with the sale of the house. Doris finally came to her senses and agreed to have Mrs. Cason sell the house. We all signed the sales contract.

The Bible says, Every wise woman buildeth her house, but the foolish plucketh it down with her hands (Proverbs 14: 1).

How true that is!

The house sold, I paid off the lawyer, and after thinking about all the injustice that had happened, went to the library and started studying law.

I still wanted my family back, but a lot of damage had been done, and the targeting wouldn't allow it.

I tried anyway.

I filed an appeal to the divorce decree within the thirty-day filing period. I noted the commissioner made an error in his ruling about awarding my wife over 50% of the present value of my retirement and how it violated the standards in Va. Code, Section 20-107.3.g. They did this to keep Doris happy and not come back. And they gave her $1500.00 and custody of Sarah.

Finally, I was scheduled to get my case in front of an appeals judge, but at the last moment they canceled my hearing!

Everything normal, I thought. Three elders from the church had agreed to go with me.

Further attempts on my life did little to discourage me.

A man in a beat up car swerved in front of me on the I-264 entrance ramp as I went downtown to mail another set of briefs.

We merged onto a deserted freeway and he nearly hit me as he passed. Then he slowed and nearly bumped me out of my lane.

I slowed trying to stay away from the nut and now we're down to 30 mph. This scene took place at 2:00 in the afternoon on a normally busy road but today there is no traffic.

These perpetrators have the connections to hold up traffic on toll roads, and the toll booths were just a couple miles behind me.

Maybe this nut following me banged them up and they are cleaning up the mess, I think. *Now nobody can drive on the expressway any longer. Or maybe the two lawyers have managed to clear the road for this game.*

But I know now the perpetrators can tie up machines at tolling booths with their direct energy, just as well as they can manipulate voting machines.

Anyway, I continued on about 20 mph behind him, just knowing somebody would rear end me, but there was no traffic for the next four miles! I exited at the downtown ramp to go to the Post Office, but I took an opposite turn and pulled in under a ramp of a parking garage.

Maybe the nut will go past me, I thought.

Twenty minutes passed and the road was clear, so I continued on my way to the Post Office to mail the court brief.

For the second time, Court of Appeals would look at my brief. However, during that period, one judge announced his retirement, and the next day my request for a re-hearing was denied.

I filed another appeal, but with the Supreme Court of Virginia a month later, and another judge resigned, citing personal problems, but the paper had the judge criticizing unworthy lawyers.

I got a good look at the nut fronting me that day on the interstate and I remembered his face.

Approximately one month later, a driver decided to pass me on the right hand side of a residential road as I traveled to work early one morning. This time he was driving a police car, and he stared icily ahead as he went by me at 5: 45 a.m.

The policeman could have taken driving lessons from my former attorney. My attorney on two occasions would pull out in front of me at 5:00 in the morning as I made my way to work. He lived about 12 miles from me, so what was he doing in my area at that time of the morning?

But there he would be, in his old green car, pulling out in front of me several days throughout the week for a two-month period. At this time, I made a complaint about him to the Va. State Bar because I wanted my retirement fixed.

And he had even written in the decree that my retirement was disposable!

That wording would be crossed out. I had not worked for the federal government for ten years during my marriage.

One time my lawyer was standing with two policemen beside their cars on the side of the road at 5:30 a.m. I guess this was his way of intimidating me into dropping my complaint. But after learning about the hologram projection, I sense this was a projection that would try and make me look nuts if I complained.

Later, I talked to a few lawyers in town about helping me out; with many of the offices I had visited becoming vacant within a couple of months.

Mail addressed to these two lawyers then started coming across my letter carrier case but neither of the lawyers lived on my route, nor had they offices on my route.

And who was the dark-skinned black haired man who had walked through the swinging back doors of the Post Office where I worked and asked my fellow carriers where my distribution case was! That's right, right through the doors of an unprotected federal facility.

Dressed in black pants with a white open shirt collar, he walked out just as I arrived at 5:55 a.m. and he went to the parking lot to get in his late model black Cadillac with a D.C. plate on the front and no plate on the back.

And then I got warned about what had happened to a carrier a few cases from me: he just had an operation for a pinched nerve. He was obviously practice for them, and then they would target me. This is a common practice by the perpetrators – to make sure their targeting works before they put it on the real victim.

Further attempts on my life continued. I came home to find someone had broken the glass at the back door and been in the apartment.

Then a noise started penetrating my apartment to the point I couldn't sleep. I was a mail carrier walking several miles a day. I had to have my sleep.

At the same time, someone would start stalking me on my route. A mailman knows about things happening on his route!

And a man in the late model car would stare at me and drive off insanely erratic. Somehow the perpetrators would also target my postal vehicle.

They were trying to drive me insane or kill me.

I was being attacked at my carrier case, on the route, and now at my apartment.

Unable to sleep in the house for nights, I started sleeping in my car, as many victims have had to, because the metal helps protect a person.

The noises continued in my apartment and a knot developed on the back of my neck.

I had not slept in days and I was still trying to work. And I was feeling ill.

Are they aiming something at me here also? They can't get anything on me, so now they are trying to kill me.

I had to do something, because evil was surrounding me.

Depart From Evil

God hath delivered me to the ungodly, and turned me over into the hands of the wicked. I was at ease, but he hath broken me asunder; he hath also taken me by my neck, and shaken me to pieces, and set me up for his mark.

His archers compass me round about; he cleaveth my kidneys asunder, and doth not spare; he poureth out my gall upon the ground. He breaketh me with breach upon breach; he runneth upon me like a giant. I have sewed sackcloth upon my skin, and defiled my strength in the dust. My face is foul with weeping, and on my eyelids is the shadow of death; Not for my violence in mine hands. Also my prayer is pure.

O earth, cover not thou my blood, and let my cry have no place. Also now, behold, my witness is in heaven, and my record is on high. My friends scorn me, but mine eye poureth out tears unto God. Ho, that one might plead for a man with God, as a man pleadeth for his neighbor!

When a few years are come, then I shall go the way from which I shall not return. (Job 16: 11-22).

The knot on my neck got bigger. Three terrible days passed; I was stressed out.

The oxygen to my brain slowed, from the tightening of the muscles.

I arrived home from work the third or fourth day around 4:00 p.m. as I usually did, ate some dinner, and tried to rest, but again, something targeted me. And I continued to remember about the glass being broken on the door above the door.

I couldn't take it: I walked around the lake that surrounded an apartment complex in the back of my unit; and it was the first time I had the helicopter experience and stalking many victims complain about, other than a few months before this period when I started playing ball for the church softball team and one continued to hover over the field for some reason.

When I walked back to the apartment area, I saw my trial court's judge car in my neighborhood!

The license plate with his initials on it were clear.

I knew something was crazy, and I began to get scared. I mean, the man lived miles away from my dead end neighborhood, and I certainly didn't blame him for anything: he had ruled in my favor.

The fourth night, on a Thursday I believe, at sunset, I looked for answers.

God speaks in dark places, and I looked for a quiet place to pray.

I found a patch of woods about a block down the road, made my way around broken bottles, pine trees, and litter, and sat down to seek God's counsel. Surely no one would bother me here.

The woods hardly offered a quiet place because they were next to a busy four lane road, but I needed somewhere to think, and then I remembered the prayer chapel up at the Rock Church.

Maybe it was open.

So I decided to go.

It was getting late. The sun had gone down but it was my only desire.

I entered the chapel and found my way upstairs to the dark prayer room.

But what would I be praying for?

We don't always know until trouble comes, and then God intercedes as He has for centuries of time to those that love Him.

Safety was on my mind.

The words from Psalms 37: 27 echoed throughout me:
Depart from evil, and do good; and dwell for evermore

I knew the evil perpetrators wanted me gone, and I would never submit to intimidation, but when God decrees something, it's time to do it.

I really think those words relate to personal evil, but at this moment, they were meant for me to leave the area for safety. So I would make my plan to escape evil and Virginia.

The other thing that came to my mind was about how faithful people in Hebrews 11: 34 had escaped the edge of the sword. They went out away from terror not knowing where they were going but went on faith to find a better place.

Who through faith, subdued kingdoms, wrought righteousness, obtained promises, stopped the mouths of lions . . . and these all, having received witness through faith received not the promise, God having provided some better thing for us, that they without us should not be made perfect (Hebrews 11: 33-40).

After all, I had just exposed corruption in the Norfolk court system, a law firm that was exploiting its own clients, and false businesses that were set up to harass people. I didn't ask for all this – it just began to surround me.

So where would I stay in the meantime until I got my belongings together?

I could not go home. But I decided to tackle that issue after work the next day. I would try and make it one more day.

The next day after work, instead of going home, I again went to a place I knew would be quiet: the grounds of my old Junior High School at Lake Taylor. But before I got there, I picked up a newspaper.

Sitting out in the middle of the field and seeing that all was clear around me, I found what I was looking for: *Room for Rent, $25.00 per week.*

90

I drove and found a pay phone and made the call.

"Sure, you can stay here. Come on over. The rent is $100.00/month."

I made my way over to Martha's house in Virginia Beach and that's where I would stay for about a month.

I didn't think it was that unusual that Air Force planes would be flying over my bedroom because Oceana Naval Air Station is a very busy base, but now I know it was programmed to harass me. Once every forty-five seconds a plane would come over my bedroom for hours.

This went on quite a few nights just as a same scenario would occur years later in Jacksonville, N.C. as I was building a shed on a lot. They continually dove down over my work area no more than a couple hundred feet all throughout the days of the week I was there. That was no coincidence.

And now a private hearse would crisscross a neighboring street as I walked around the block.

As the years went by, I sensed the Joint Armed Service Command was behind many of these attacks, and their training office was located just off Military Highway.

Anyway, Martha's house gave me some relief, but I was still being targeted.

I made it to church one Sunday but I was a mess, not having hardly any sleep.

After a few days of being at Martha's, I finally got nerve to go back over to the old apartment and gather the rest of my belongings one weekend.

I made more plans to leave the area.

I had not the foggiest idea of how I would pay my child support of $150.00 every two weeks if I left and quit the Post Office, but I knew I couldn't pay it if I were dead.

I took my last thousand dollars and bought a station wagon to haul my personal belongings, and Martha had a garage where I could lock the car up at night.

I would quit work at the end of the month, terminate my lease at the old apartment, and get out of the Tidewater area.

On a Friday afternoon at 4:00 p.m., sometime in September of 1990, I left my native homeland of the Tidewater area.

On my way out of town, I stopped near downtown Norfolk to say goodbye to an angel who had stuck by me for three years, a beloved sister of God, who nursed my emotions and comforted me with her faith.

It wasn't unusual to see five times as many state troopers on the roads that night. So it wasn't unusual for a state police helicopter to come out of nowhere and hover over my car the last twenty miles to the North Carolina state line.

What a waste of money! These perpetrators should be made to repay the state for all the unwarranted actions taken against innocent citizens. Materials, equipment, manpower, and paperwork have been unnecessarily expended.

Twenty miles *across* the state line at the first rest stop, I stopped and thanked the Lord for delivering me from evil.

As I tried to get a nap, a prostitute knocked on my window and asked, "Can I help you this evening?"

The area was much too close to Virginia, so I drove another fifty miles to find rest near Greensboro.

Cherokee Refuge

Rays from the sun awoke me as I found myself slumped over in the front seat of the car at a rest stop near Greensboro, North Carolina.

My goods were overflowing into the front seat, but the station wagon I had purchased was a good thing; there was plenty of room for things important to me.

Groggily, I exited the car and took a walk—still wondering what the hell I had been through not only for the last four years since I had left Cherokee, but especially during the last month.

The knot on the back of my neck now was about an inch in circumference. I figured it was from stress on the nerves, but knowing what I know now, I was more than likely implanted right before the craziness started in July.

I got back in the car and drove five more hours to exit the familiar cutoff to Cherokee. This time, I would not be driving back.

Thirty minutes later, I stopped at a familiar shopping center in Waynesville. It was dusk, and the view from the parking lot of the setting sun over the mountains was awesome. Lots of land was visible. As I scanned the horizon, I thought again about what had happened, where I was coming from, and where I was going. It all seemed so senseless and confusing.

Sitting there in the parking lot for an hour brought me painful memories: a hearse that circled the house at late hours; the Virginia Beach policeman that tailgated my car for two miles just after I had visited the FCC trying to figure out who was cyber stalking me, and the four men blocking the exit door in a small foyer when I was trying to deliver mail near ODU University; and there had been five times as many state troopers on the road the night I left; and some helicopter followed me to the state line.

I got back in the car after getting a snack at the grocery store and drove over Soco Mountain to mom's house.

I greeted her and then went straight to bed. When I awoke, I still felt confused and dizzy. I thought, *Oh no, not again! This is the place where I always get better, not worse!*

This is the place where I would come to get well from the wounds in life, and now someone has seen fit to come here. This is where I recovered from a debilitating leg injury and nursed myself back to health in 1981, and the place where I recovered from hernia surgery. The sound of the running creek below the front yard gave me peace, and the flowering trees on the mountainside shed their sweet aroma on me.

What is causing this dizziness?

I tried to put the aggravation aside and enjoy the day but the dizziness continued. As I lay in bed, an airplane could be heard in the far distance, something I had never heard before at mother's house. Shortly thereafter, the room felt like it was swaying. I knew the disturbance was external.

I knew me, and I had great knowledge about how to heal naturally, but I would at least make an appointment with a chiropractor in Waynesville to look at the knot on my neck, but in the middle of my thoughts; at least then I would be able substantiate why I left my job.

It would be more than just the planes that would be seeking my whereabouts. As mom and I were driving her car to the chiropractor's office in Waynesville, a late model black Ford car began to follow us. The car was quite noticeable in the middle of autumn on the Reservation four-lane highway where there's hardly any traffic in November – before the casino came to town.

94

I slowed down, and he slowed down. So I stopped right in the middle of the road. He did a U-turn and disappeared.

Mom later told me the FBI asked for permission to conduct surveillance of her phone conversations, but this guy wasn't a FBI guy.

Six weeks passed and I felt much better. The knot went down on the back of my neck and I began to eat decent food. But now I was in need of money, to make the support payments for Sarah.

The sick leave pay from the Post Office would help but I wanted to go to work – somewhere. I was not going back to Norfolk after the murder attempt.

Fortune came my way, and in early March, I got a temporary job with the Bureau of Indian Affairs Fire Crew. This only lasted three weeks, but it did a lot for my morale after what I had been through. I was physically active – and I was going to church.

And then in April, I was able to get a seasonal job with the Park Service. By letter, I quit the Post Office, after an argument about them not doing enough to protect me from direct energy attacks as I was casing my mail. Someone had used direct energy on me at that Thomas Corner Post Office; they had disturbed me while I was carrying the mail, and they saw fit to manipulate the Inspectors to harass me.

I should have figured something was going on when one of the carriers suddenly went down with a pinched nerve and went into surgery, arrived weeks later with a brace on his neck. He was their practice guy. His case was about five cases down from me, and he had been in good physical condition.

And then new supervisors would be brought in from other cities. These supervisors I did not know, and they began to treat me roughly, going so far as to hide behind bushes and catch me driving my postal vehicle fifty yards with my door open on a hot day to give me a ticket and take my license. They took me off my regular route and put me on a walking route – right behind the Post Office – where the perpetrators could continue to target me from the apartments in back of the Post Office.

Starting Over Again

Sensing I may be coming to Cherokee one day, I had bought a small lot just across the county line about three miles from mom's house. I had already installed a septic tank.

Anyway, I started building a shed -- to learn more about construction for one thing. One day while working on it, I received a call from the Park Service on a telephone I had installed in the shed.

They offered me work in the summer months. This job was something I really needed! There weren't many decent paying jobs around Cherokee.

I started working at Deep Creek campground. It was a seasonal job but one that would at least pay the bills.

And then I bought a mobile home. It wasn't much of one, but it would be mine and I could shield myself somewhat better than if I was at mom's house.

After getting my trailer set up, I was still receiving pulsations hitting my body. Trying to determine the source, I bought several pieces of electronic equipment. One day, while listening to a Citizens Band radio, which only picked up broadcasts nearby since mountains surrounded the trailer, I heard, "He's got a radio!"

I suspected someone at the Recreational Vehicle Park 100 yards below my trailer was now monitoring my actions and stalking me. Searching around my home, I found a stash of stomped out cigarettes behind a bush fifty yards away from my kitchen window.

One of the things perpetrators do is loosen wires like the neutral and ground wires, or disconnect them from their proper places and put them near a hot wire – where pulsing will occur throughout the circuit. I doubt it's a coincidence 18 serviceman died over in Iraq from electrocution, some in the bathroom shower and others in a swimming pool, from a report I read.

It's bad enough radiological frequencies are disturbing the human nervous system through regular household wiring and the smart meters, for many victims have proved that.

A person would want to make sure the electrical panel is bonded to a good ground. If there is still a problem, have the resistance composition of your soil checked out to make sure there is a good ground.

For what it's worth, I've wired houses from start to finish, having been schooled at a vocational school in Norfolk while attending the tenth grade.

Anyway, the targeting continued. Air Force planes would suddenly descend from the sky and come down over my property -- their emanations cutting off my ground fault electrical breaker and causing severe pain to my body. And whenever I traveled, a small plane would appear just as I arrived somewhere or went somewhere – I presume to get my coordinates.

The harassment was so bad one night, after I had been at the trailer for a couple of years that I called my friend Miriam and asked if I could spend the night with her.

A Friend

I had met Miriam at church, and I knew her husband had recently separated from her and was banned from her property because he'd get drunk and beat her constantly.

Miriam trusted me, and she welcomed me over the house. Miriam had two kids: one was a two-month old baby girl at home; and the other was about seven years old at grandma's house.

Miriam wasn't really capable of watching children because she had terrible temper tantrums and a childish personality. So I welcomed the responsibility of watching the toddler. Both kids had different fathers, who did not claim responsibility for either of them.

The situation worked out well. The young one needed a dad and I needed a place to stay. And Miriam needed somebody to cut wood and do odd jobs. But everybody in town was talking about the guy who moved in with Miriam. Everyone knows everything in Cherokee. It's all family, and quite a few people lined the road one day as I drove up to the house.

I thought possibly building a log cabin back at the trailer site would protect me from some of the non-ionizing radiation fields the perpetrators were targeting me with from the campground. I had always wanted a cabin, and so I began building such things as cabinets and furniture in the cold winter months at Miriam's house so they would be ready to go in the cabin.

I stayed with Miriam about five years, enjoying the kids and continuing to work at the Park Service.

One summer, I built a rock garden wall about 20 inches high that stretched out about 40 feet overlooking the cove below the house. I used creek sand and everything from mud rock and field stone to make the double wall.

Miriam's house was backed up against a mountain, so this was another good refuge for me, and I'm certain God had supplied this residence to keep me protected. Naturally it bothered me that she was in the middle of a separation, but she eventually got a divorce.

I knew the time would come when I would be leaving Miriam. Staying there was not my destiny. I wanted to write and finish my cabin. But I did have a wonderful time with the kids.

I didn't think it strange however, after I had made reservations for all of us to see an Atlanta Braves baseball game, that ten minutes before the game we were all told it might be cancelled, because of a fire which burned up the press box.

I can go on and on with stories like these that were examples of just how far these perpetrators will go to deny a victim's happiness. Other victims will tell you the same thing.

Anyway, terrible things went on around the mountains that were kept quiet, for fear of scaring tourists away.

I came home to the house one day to find Miriam crying and in pain. Her brother had raped her, and apparently had been doing it over the years. I took her to the police station to file a complaint, which she did, and they went looking for the brother. He hid out for a few days, and eventually he was able to get the complaint withdrawn after a couple of months because he had a cousin on the police force.

Anyway, while I was at Miriam's house, I sold my trailer and began building the cabin. I built the perimeter block foundation, installed plumbing lines, and had the concrete slab poured. The 6 x 8 inch white logs were being shaped and the trusses were on their way. Once everything was delivered, I had a crew of five guys to help me get the logs up and roof on.

I suppose my perpetrators saw what I was doing, and the last thing they wanted was me being on my own again, free of people they could manipulate against me; so just about the time I was getting ready to leave, Miriam's ex-husband showed up in the neighborhood and threatened me. A couple of months earlier, my rear window of the car was smashed out.

It was time to go back home.

My Cabin

I packed up my car with my clothes and moved in my cabin though it still had a lot of work to be done. But I had installed the shower, toilet, and sink. And the windows and doors were installed, so the place was livable.

I had one electrical line from the outside temporary power receptacle that would furnish electricity if I needed. For heat, I had a wood stove I got from the Qualla Housing Authority auction for $35.00. My water heater I got free from a trade magazine listing near Asheville. That was a mistake getting that because it was an old heater that was full of rust.

I enjoyed working on the house: installing the 1" x 6" white pine ceiling and walls, tile floor, and making my own doors from 2" x 8: planks. It was a true log cabin.

But my targeting would continue in earnest.

Further attempts on my life left me questioning the motives of a loving God in my journal.

Coming home one day to a frying pan with poison on the inside of it made me cringe. One morning the oatmeal had an alkali substance in it. And I would have ammonia exiting my nose from the perpetrators contamination – all in attempt to try and pattern the targeting of my father with ammonia poisoning.

One night at a Chinese restaurant the smell of ammonia hovered over my food on the table. It's not a coincidence my father nearly died from ammonia poisoning. Maybe the devil thinks it will look alright if I do too.

The ammonia is not coming from the cleaning man's mop bucket. The ammonia is on the crab legs. Other guests complain about it. There was plenty of time for the devil to make his plans, because I had discussed where we were going in the car.

I once came home and began to drink water from one of the water jugs, but the taste gripped my throat. It was more ammonia, and I went to the bathroom and vomited.

The perpetrators will often look into a family's past and try to kill a person with something that has killed the parents.

One night after taking one of the local kids to a Hornets game in Charlotte, I found myself beating on the steering wheel to the music, and then I remembered I had left the Apple juice on my car seat while I was at the game, and then I had some of it. After getting home, I laid on the floor for days being delirious from the poisoning wondering if I would live.

Prior to that, months earlier, while playing tennis with Miriam's nine year old, Tasha, in Waynesville, a man sped off in a car just as we were about to finish our tennis match. After drinking some juice I had left in the car, I then knew he had drugged it. I wondered if I would make it back over the mountain in the car.

If all that wasn't enough, they implanted my stomach at a time when I was apparently asleep. I have implants around the navel area and both sides of the chest areas.

I suppose they were now trying to emulate the oat cell cancer my father got.

Another hard spot is on the right side near my hip. The implants would begin to exit years later, in the form of black specks – seeds – as one targeted friend up north would call them. And now I'm rather sure about the leg injury that occurred years earlier from running and prolonged standing – there was a bump area right in the femoral nerve area in the crease of the groin.

In 2014, I found toxic black implants under the skin at strategic nerve places all over my body, and needle marks – places like at the top of the feet, armpits, four

103

around the heart area of the left chest, knee muscles, inner thighs, bottom of the spine where a rare earth magnet managed to heat them and cause them to expand into a surface issue.

I'd be awakened at times in the night by airplanes and God knows what else in the skies and space: I questioned my commitment to the Lord.

My journal says, I sit in a state of perpetual fear, because I wonder how long the murder attempts will continue: There are persecutions now, but I am not forsaken.

The targeting drove me closer to the Lord, and I would continue to attend church. One day I met a beautiful woman at the Pentecostal Church. She was so talented: she could sing, make crafts, and care for those who needed it. Her mother and mine had gone to school together. But anyway, Amanda and I would spend much time together making patch quilts, hiking the trails, and playing board games. This was a great encouragement for me, for she was a spiritually strong Cherokee woman.

The Lord brought another fine person into my life about this time, Madeline Owl, who used to make baskets and jewelry at the Indian Village. Madeline was older and needed some assistance, so I would pick her up and take her to church.

When things got crazy, I would spend lots of time with Madeline at her house – making beadwork, reading scriptures, and cooking food. After all, the perpetrators had turned my family against me. But Madeline took me in as her child. She was nearly full blood Cherokee. Our silence each evening spoke feelings of abuse from the foreigners that plagued our lives.

I felt terrible however one cold December evening, when I had taken some kids I had maintained contact with shopping over the mountain. The next day I heard that Madeline had fallen outside her door trying to get firewood. She could not get back up, and she died.

About this time in 1997 I had had enough of the Park Service. I wasn't getting anywhere at being promoted to a full-time job. I had made a couple of errors at work and the boss would hold them against me forever. But I was being bothered by someone who was still stalking me.

But I was a very good worker and very well respected until the targeting worsened.

I was the one who always went on jobs to help the other journeyman. So I gained lots of knowledge about plumbing, masonry, electricity, and carpentry during this time, especially being on a re-modeling crew where each member interacted in all the building activities. This knowledge helped me build my cabin. I'm certain I was being groomed for the superintendent's job, but the targeting made things terrible.

Leaving the Government

Seeing that the perpetrators were ruining my life at the Park Service, I decided to leave and find another job. After all, I had been first on the list to receive a permanent job three times but each time the job would be reverted or abolished.

So in 1997 after seven years with the Park Service, I left my seasonal job for a maintenance job at the Cherokee Holiday Inn. I stayed there a year. I became interested in heating and air conditioning. So I went to school and got certified to be able to recover refrigerants.

When the test was finally scheduled to get certified, the perpetrators tired me considerably the previous two nights, so when I was going to take the test, I was extremely tired.

Rounding a curve, at one of their marked intersections, I fell asleep in the car and hit an oncoming vehicle at about 20 mph. The fatalities could have been bad, but fortunately, only the cars were damaged.

I ended up one point short with a "69" score on the test and would have to take it again a couple of months later, and I passed.

I then took a job with a couple of heating and air contractors, but both jobs fell through for one reason or another, and both contractors indicated to me they were targeted in one way or another.

One said, "You know. They always stay one step ahead of me."

The other contractor would suffer a heart attack shortly after I quit.

I was jobless in May of 1998, but it was golf weather, and that's where I headed for two months. And I wanted to add a room on the cabin.

This is a time when I should be enjoying my life, so I found a little pool room over the mountain in Waynesville, where I would spend many nights in the next few years playing pool on the nine-foot tables.

Benney operated a pool room and kept the tables immaculate: he managed a clean room with no alcohol and drinks. This was heaven to me, because I spent lots of time playing pool in Norfolk at the bowling alley a couple miles from the house at Fox Hall. And I played quite a bit at the bars in Norfolk.

But Benney was one great pool player that kept his fame in his room. He did venture out and win the Smoky Mountain Nine Ball Open, a tournament he started to help disadvantaged kids.

Benney would easily have fifty bucks in his pocket after a few hours of a ring game of nine-ball. I would always have my five or ten to the good after the shooting was over. But Benney could beat anyone. He was a shooter who could easily run three or four racks of balls on a table with very tight pockets. I could beat him in eight ball, maneuver around him with a safety or two, but never outshoot him. And if I did, my perpetrators would hit me with adverse energy to mess up my game. This would happen usually after the fifth game or so when I was winning. But I was very good.

I started going to national tournaments, and the perpetrators would see me gaining momentum going into the fourth round; they would hit me with adverse energy and mess things up.

I played the South Carolina amateur champion and had a chance to win but I got targeted heavily. Running out my first rack to the eight ball in a nine ball game, I missed an easy angle shot. I lost my concentration because I could feel the forces around changing. I knew it was the perpetrators.

He went on to run three racks. I got my chance and again missed another easy shot after pocketing eight of the balls.

It was an easy shot but my targeting affected me; so I had to give up the national tournaments as a result.

But I loved going to Waynesville and shooting pool. Four of us played several times a week and I easily pocketed a couple thousand dollars over a few years.

Needing a real job after building my addition, I headed over to the newly built casino in Cherokee.

I was sure I could get in maintenance, but they wanted me to start out on a cleaning crew first. They said after ninety days I would be able to put in a for a maintenance job. I was scheduled for the graveyard shift, four days a week, including weekends.

It was a great job, just sweeping and picking up drink cups. It was fun. And I eventually talked my boss into letting me roll the garbage can around to pick up trash from floor cans.

This job would enable me to write my first devotional book in the daytime, and I would work at the casino at night.

God's Help Now had originated in my heart during the late 1980's as I was working as a training technician of the Post Office. I would come across all kinds of personalities with all kinds of problems, and wanting to be a great instructor, I felt burdened to help each person pass their tests and qualify for whatever position they were applying.

I found that turning to the scriptures helped me deal with each individual. I had no one else to turn to.

I felt myself grow spiritually as well. Seeing uneducated and some handicapped people moved by the good Lord to pass tests they had no business passing, I knew it was God who had the answers to succeed.

I have always had a special intimacy with God since I have been an isolated targeted individual most of my life: He was the only one I could fully trust. It worked for me, and I supposed God has used me to help others.

I would continue to give God glory by writing this self-help book but first I wanted to make sure people would read my writing.

So I started out writing and submitting devotions to publishing companies. I didn't get one accepted until 1999, on Christmas Eve of all days, by The Upper Room. Then I submitted some stories to magazine companies and one got selected by *Mountain Ideas* for publication. And then a new political newspaper started up, and I would get $25 for each story printed. All these submissions helped build my confidence for writing a book of devotions. Though many devotions got rejected by magazine editors, I held onto them, knowing that God had a purpose for each of them.

I discovered I had a lot of work to do, because some did not sound good at all, and I was still getting targeted.

But between some friends at the casino and the members of a local writing group in James, I was getting better as a writer, something the devil did not want to happen.

Some of the devotions were written twenty times. Others I would throw away and start over with a new story. After two years, I completed the seventy-one devotions and found a printer in Johnson City Tennessee to print the book.

I also found a truck coming straight at me in my lane going up Balsam Mountain, when I was going to pick up my books.

Janet

There were two night shift cleaning crews at the casino and their schedules overlapped on Wednesday nights. On the first Wednesday night, I started sweeping the floor with the other workers, until the garbage cans filled, and then I would empty them into a bigger container at the rear of the building.

While I was sweeping again, a girl working in one of our purple uniforms from the other crew caught my attention near the pot-of-gold machines on the river side of the casino. It was the same girl at Rose's I had seen a year earlier as I was checking out goods at the cash register.

Janet was a 47 year old woman who was handicapped somewhat with smaller than usual feet and a slight limp, but she had a great attitude. She had never been out on a date with a guy. She was living with her sister and father, whose health was failing.

Janet had some other physical problems; she would at times turn white as a ghost, and she would stutter her words. She could hardly carry on a conversation for any length of time -- just move on and giggle. I kept working at her, hoping one day to take her out on a date.

Meanwhile, everybody in the casino was talking about the guy who's trying to start something with Janet. They were just trying to protect her.

The more I talked to her, the more sensible she became. There was nothing wrong with this girl. She had just been overprotected, and nobody had shown sincere interest in her. But I liked her, and she showed interest back to me, and before long we were escaping to a private sanctuary outside the employee's cafeteria and enjoying laughing with each other.

Janet was physically cold when I first met her. Her hands would be freezing. Her blood pressure was very low, and I figured her to live a maximum of five years at the rate she was going.

But I got her to start eating better and I massaged some of those bone joints to get some blood circulating in her legs. After a couple of months, her color held, and she warmed up. Where before she constantly complained about low blood pressure, she now hardly said anything about it and looked forward to eating new foods I introduced to her.

She now eats healthy nutritious meals, and she's stronger than she's ever been. She also gained ten pounds, which she needed, because she only weighed 99 pounds when I met her. She got up to 110 and was looking good. After a couple of months of flirting with her, I finally got a date with her.

We went to go to the Western North Carolina Fair that is held every September at Asheville. This would be Janet's first date, and I was ecstatic because I knew she was one in a million. Everybody had told me how sweet she was, but I had no idea of the love she had in her heart.

As we ascended the hill to see the livestock show, she grabbed my hand and held tight. I put her family worries aside, her dad's failing health and her overprotective sister. And I went about my business of getting to know Janet better.

Our relationship blossomed into one of laughter, learning, togetherness, a few disagreements, and love— and on her birthday I gave her an engagement ring, after I had asked her to marry me a couple of months earlier. She gave it back a few weeks later, but I refused it, which was probably a big mistake. I had no idea this was another programmed marriage, but I was beginning to catch on.

Her family thought I had gotten her pregnant. So they would take her to the doctor and get her examined against her will. Then they made up all kinds of stories about me, telling her I would be a bad match because I was divorced, usually jobless, and that I was after sex.

No problem: I've been slandered, defamed, and rejected all my life, so it was nothing unusual to hear.

Sylva NC

I had a vision of moving to Sylva, North Carolina many years prior to moving there. In fact, I had forgotten all about the vision until I got there! Now I'm pretty certain this was part of the programming.

But I had visited Sylva in 1986 and thought it was a place where I wanted to live. It had a nice library, old houses with private settings on hilly streets, and lots of nice people.

But after the casino came to Cherokee, Sylva changed. In came Wal-Mart, Lowe's, and some national food chains. Then hurricanes would drive a flock of Floridians to stay at their mountain homes permanently. The traffic increased four- fold.

But all this happened after I had made the decision to sell my cabin and move to Sylva, so Janet and I could be closer to her family. Little did I know the extent of stalking that would happen.

The perpetrators would have a much easier time to get at me in this new neighborhood years later.

But anyway, about this time is when I decided to marry Janet, and besides, someone had broken in my cabin and stole my television.

I put my cabin up for sale. It sold the next day after I had put up a sign just off Route 441. I got the $68,000 for my cabin and bought an older home just outside the city limits of Sylva, a great place, because now I would be closer to the golf course, the pool room in Waynesville, Janet, a town, the library, and my church in James. But I would be out of my last $2,000.

That said, I still had the burden to find money to publish my book, and one day my prayers were answered.

Mom stepped in and gave me the $3200 to have 1000 copies printed.

It didn't surprise me on the day I went to get my books at Johnson City Tennessee a truck would be heading straight at me as I was ascended the first mountain from Sylva. It was going about 75 miles per hour and had crossed the center median. The driver was asleep at the wheel.

The truck would speed by me on my far right hugging the guard rail, and I would look in my rear view mirror to see it continue down the hill only to spin in the middle of the road and come to a stop. I continued on, knowing that this was just another attempt to roadblock success. There were people stopping to assist.

After picking up the books, I was able to sell nearly 500 over the next few years.

Meanwhile, since I was making a move, I wanted a job closer to home. Western Carolina University hired me as a bookstore clerk. What a contrast from being a cleaner at the casino. Everyone was so serious at this bookstore, and my supervisor threatened me one day because I was finding new ways to do things to make jobs much easier.

Finally, I quit and decided to go back to maintenance work. I got hired at a non-profit facility that made hygienic pads for medical facilities. That job too only lasted about three months because they fired me at the ninety day period. This is the first time I had ever been fired from a job. It certainly wasn't because of my performance. I was fixing everything around there! And the supervisor hated it.

I had enough, seeing me get cheated out of three good jobs at the Park Service, the maintenance position at the Casino because I did not have enough Indian blood, and now these last two jobs where I'm sure the circumstances were manipulated to make me look bad.

So I went out on my own.

I headed immediately to my computer, made up business cards stating I was available for maintenance work, and then passed them around at the hardware stores and real estate offices. I put an ad in the paper and then took my last $700.00 and bought a truck from a private owner at Maggie Valley though the undersides were rusting out. I got my tools loaded and waited for a call.

The local hardware sales lady mentioned my name to a woman who needed her house painted, and I ended up working for Mrs. Richards off and on for the next five years. What a blessing!

And then Mr. Thurmond with a real estate company began to call and I would fix many problems in his rental units. It was good money. And then other calls started to come in.

This new job threw off my perpetrators somewhat because I could schedule my work as I pleased; however, say if I went to a remote location in the country, Air Force planes would immediately come swooping down just after I got set up working, especially when I set up an aluminum ladder. Swaying on the ladder due to their targeting, I had to come up with something to stabilize me and get rid of the targeting. I painted the ladder black, and that helped a great deal.

For many years, a smaller plane would first locate my coordinates whenever I arrived or went somewhere, and then the jets would follow. And, at or near 4: 30 p.m. every day, regardless of where I was at, the small plane would fly overhead. I could be a hundred miles in any direction and that smaller plane with its distinct motor sound would fly overhead.

Friday afternoon around 2:30 would also be a consistent targeting exercise. I could feel the forces move around me. I suppose they were setting me up for the weekend. The energy would target my head.

Anyway, my self-employed maintenance job went great for about six years, until all those hurricanes occurred in Florida and many people came back to their summer homes in the mountains. Most of those people must have been handymen. There had been only a couple of us handymen in Jackson County, and suddenly there were many more.

I knew the perpetrators were also capable of destroying relationships. As I stated before, I had become friends with a wonderful Christian Indian woman and watched as the perpetrators would target her kids to use drugs, tell lies, and steal. The younger son would eventually kill someone in a few years. The same boy who would sit quietly in church pulled the trigger to kill a girl. And then the perpetrators would try and entangle me in some kind of abuse scheme with the woman's daughter, who often stayed over at my cabin. Sensing the evil, I broke off my relationship with the woman, but we had many happy days hunting ginseng, quilting blankets, and gardening. She just didn't understand the targeting process and how it used people against each other.

But I certainly didn't know the extent they would go to break up my marriage. I was still learning about this targeting mess.

Janet and I got married on April 20, 2001, at a beautiful ceremony at Lake Junaluska Methodist Assembly Center where a cross sits above the lake. Our first year was great, but then Janet started being with her sister more and more on her days off. She was not acting the same as the she had the previous four years we had known each other. I was doing everything to appease her, attending her home church, visiting her family, and taking her wherever she wanted. But suddenly she turned against me.

Now I know my perpetrators were setting me up with another divorce. This is what they do, manipulate couples to get married, and separate them with mood frequencies. They have the power to create such feelings, along with sexual feelings at other than ordinary times.

Many victims testify of this – about electromagnetic radiation fields that cause the blood to go to the lower parts of the body for stimulation, Couple that with the exotic images and voices they can send to the head – and they put people together that really don't have natural feelings towards each other. Hear of it all the time. Targeted victims now look back in their history and know many of their relationships were manipulated by a third party to take place. Evil.

This reminds me of a book I just read, Tamara, the lone survivor of a hurricane at sea, climbs out of the cabin to find her partner missing and the boat a mess. She breaks down and cries and wants to die -- as many normal women would want to do at that point, but she hears a voice – telling her to start bailing out water from the flooded boat. She argues with this voice and tells it to go away but it continues to issue commands, until she finally gets saved by a passing vessel.

Little did she know she was a targeted victim of the evil voice to skull technology (as what victims would refer it to). Reading book after book, I continue to see the targeting concept used on people. Bobby Fisher, who was a former world chess champion, was plagued by stalkers and electronic targeting.

He tried to escape the madness by moving to Finland to live out his years. My opinion is that he found some peace over there because cold weather shuts down some of these implants. I had the very thing happen to me at the beach one day, swimming in cold water, and surfacing to find my targeting had disappeared. I was free, for the time being, and I was extremely talkative and care free for the next few hours, until the targeting got me again. The implants had warmed up.

A bright baseball prospect was another poor victim —
confessing to a dream the perpetrators sent him and then
going to prison for it when such an event happened near
his home. He was eventually set free, but the targeting
had basically killed him in prison.

I was encouraging Janet to get a driver's license, and
one afternoon she practiced driving the car in a deserted
parking lot in Sylva. Janet drove around the parking lot
and crossed a little residential road-- as she went back
and forth through the lot. Twenty times she stopped the
car at the road and proceeded through the lot. There was
no traffic on the residential road.

Again she descended a small hill and prepared to stop
the car.

I mentioned to her, "A car is coming."

She said nothing.

I told her again and again.

"Put your foot on the brake and stop the car."

She failed to respond, as if she was in some personal
trance.

"Stop the car!" I yell.

"I can't find the brake," she says.

But her foot had been on it the whole time.

I yelled at her again, and she did nothing.

The approaching car was now about thirty feet from
us and traveling about forty miles per hour.

I threw the gearshift into park, but the car continued
to roll—right into the oncoming car. I bowed for the
impact I knew was going to happen. But all I hear was a
rip sound. The oncoming car just caught the front bumper
and pulled it off.

A second earlier and our car would have been spun
around by the frame, and we would have been dragged
down the road and probably received some serious
injuries.

I went to the junkyard and eventually got the car fixed up enough to pass inspection, but it took a lot of time and money out of my pocket.

Personally I believe the perpetrators had her frozen at the wheel and manipulated another car to come at the precise time she was going to cross the road. This has happened repeatedly among targets. Targeted individuals say they have been targeted specifically at intersections.

With Janet busy with her sister one weekend, I had a desire to fish off the coast, plus I wanted a piece of land I could go to upon retirement.

I took off to Emerald Isle NC, where I knew there was a good fishing pier and plenty of fish. This is one of the worst mistakes of my life as a targeted individual – being somewhere alone.

The Implant

I drove the eight hour trips a couple weekends, went fishing, and eventually found a good one acre lot only ½ mile from the Intra-costal Waterway. The lot was cheap because there was water covering half of it. But the ground there was solid enough I thought, and I knew there had to be a way to salvage the lot, especially at the low price of $12,000.

Sure enough, when I started clearing the lot and looking for drainage problems, I found one – a load of concrete someone had dumped into one of the drainage ditches.

I cut down trees, had the concrete removed, and built a shed. The perpetrators saw fit that I would be harassed all weekend as two Marine Corps planes would conduct training exercises over my land all during the mid-day, diving down just when I would turn my generator on. This went on for four days, but I finally finished the shed.

When I returned to the property about two months later, I really got targeted heavily. I would sleep in my shed at night, and a strong force attacked me, which I sensed was coming from a house next door on the other side of a small patch of woods. I found out it was a rental house, and some man was anxiously showing up during the night. The microwaves, or whatever, was very strong and I had to use leftover shingles to shield my body.

My lot was near the back gate of the Camp Lejeune Marine Corps base, so there were a lot of perpetrators in the area. I don't think it's a coincidence the area had toxic water at the base in Jacksonville NC, for these perpetrators use such tactic to kill Americans.

Something was obviously wrong, and now I began to suspect I was indeed implanted with a subcutaneous object designed to be activated from remote means.

Upon my research, and contact with other victims on the Internet communication forums, my suspicions were right. It was difficult to tell however what was real good advice on the forums or what were lies, so I decided to separate the bad sheep from the good sheep by writing up a petition – to stop electronically targeting humans and to terminate direct energy programs.

My petition was well received by victims, and one new signature would appear weekly, usually also giving me a story of their tortured lives. Many of the victims were from renowned families, others were uniquely talented individuals who found themselves in the middle of a bad situation, and yet others were just innocent people the devil decided to pick on.

I wrote the *Petition to Ban Direct Energy Programs and Electronic Surveillance of Humans* in 2004.

Another victim and originator of the first website for targeted victims on the Internet, the Mind Control forum, would install a link for the petition.

There were about one hundred publicly listed victims at that time on the website, and their stories corroborated my victimization. However, there were only a few victims from the Southeast U.S. The perpetrators have always tried to keep victims apart, and this is the same tactic used as of today. If victims did get together, the energy fields would be applied to cause dissension.

The victims on the Yahoo mind control forum did start visiting each other however, and thanks to Charles Schlund, a former Government Drug Enforcement employee, we also realized we had some form of implant in us.

The argument would go on night after night about the sensitivity of implants stimulating nerves. Satan was doing everything he could to stop the information flow, including torturing the victims with more energy, which is still happening today. Many people have died as a result, including Charles.

I have found implants all over my body, the most evident being at places I had suffered injuries in the past, which is where the perpetrators would place their implants, to make it look like there was a natural cause.

One implant was placed in my stomach just behind a white mark I received from an ill attempt to try and iron my clothes when I was young. Never had a hard spot there before – until I was implanted.

Don't forget the microscopic antenna - a slim piece of black carbonized material that was 7/16" long in the middle of the chips. Dr. Stinson in Waynesville, NC, would take one of the chips out years later. Another Doctor, Simpson, however would be persuaded by a red-eyed old man shortly before I entered his office for surgery to make sure he did not disturb them cutting in that same area.

There's no doubt in my mind he influenced the doctor to avoid the implant area.

As I was sitting in the parking lot about to get out of the car, the red-eyed man looked me over good from the sidewalk in front of the car, and he immediately went into the doctor's office, only to stay for a short time and exit. I would see this same fellow months later sitting in the passenger seat of a late model black Newport car with another fellow eyeing my vehicle. I happened upon them coincidentally because I had exited the far door at Wal-Mart rather than the one next to my car.

Anyway, I had told Dr. Simpson where to cut, but he cut below the area – taking out a chunk of my flesh that took a year to heal.

There would be no targeting relief. Those implants were put right where I would usually carry my golf bag, on my right shoulder, to make me think it was my golf strap rubbing against my shoulder. That would be the last time I ever visited a doctor.

Now I'm certain these sadistic perpetrators have caused my hernia in 1980, and possibly caused my debilitating leg injury at the same time, because there is an implant in that area. I remember distinctly a bump the size of a bb there.

Anyway, my petition eventually gathered over 600 signatures, and I put many of the victims together for support in the next couple of years. I was going to make an army! But there was a strange pattern developing on the petition – signers would be nowhere near each other for support. That was probably no coincidence.

Derrick Robinson was one signee, and he would eventually inherit the *Freedom from Covert Harassment* website (which from I what understand was briefly started by a girl named Silvia in New York). I actually got a call from Silvia one day who said the perpetrators were teaching her foreign languages in her head. I convinced her to abandon the targeting and get serious with her mate.

Another important website about this time was entitled something to the effect of *Global Ban of Weapons that Manipulate the Human Nervous System.*

This may have been a perpetrator site, but I turned it into a legal reference site to end the targeting after a talk with the administrator, who claimed to be a victim.

Carolyn, an activist against chem-trails, and I started listing legal references on the site with John's approval; then I got a strange phone call wanting to know information about the site, and the site suddenly disappeared. I had had a lot of good citations on there after a few months.

About this time, a fellow by the name of John Cliftoz from England contacted me and said he was being held in a psychiatric ward of a hospital against his will. He was being electronically targeted and couldn't get the police to believe him. He needed help, so I sent the Petition there along with some testimony to the head nurse and they released him. Praise the Lord.

A lot of us victims began to share telephone numbers and electronic mail addresses to communicate with each other. After about six months, these communications led to a conference call between multiple victims.

I remember the first conference call vividly. There was a lot of static electricity on the line, which was probably instigated by the perpetrators. Lynn Thomas had started the call, and there were about four of us on there. This occurred probably in 2005.

I was being targeted heavily during that week, and upon removing a window at an apartment I was working at, the glass shattered and cut my wrist. A good deal of blood came out, and I sat in my truck a good while restricting the flow. My handkerchief was covered with blood. It's not easy to tie off a kerchief with one hand so I used my teeth to finish the knot. Finally the blood flow stopped.

The perpetrators were out for blood, considering I was putting a lot of victims all over the world in communication with each other. Upon a trip to the fishing pier at Emerald Isle, North Carolina, after sleeping in the back of my truck, they got to me: I woke up with a paralyzed right side.

They had injected something into the back of my head and Eustachian tubes with their implants.

Actually, that weekend I had planned to meet one of the signers of the petition, Josie who lived in Atlantic Beach, N.C. But I think the perpetrators made a deal with her. She showed up with a turtleneck sweater on and spoke discreetly. Across the way, in an empty parking lot about a hundred yards away, sat a car with a well dressed

Arabic looking man sitting in the driver's seat – staring at his steering wheel.

It was not the first time Middle Eastern type individuals had been in my vicinity. For when I was working for Ms. Richards in Sylva, two "art students" would suddenly rent two of her apartment units. These students had to be in their late 20's. I wasn't tipped off to the magnitude of this problem until I thought about the Western North Carolina bookstore where I worked a few years earlier – and a foreign art student would happen to be in my area quite often. And then I read about the Israeli art student spies in the United States gathering information about politicians. When I had a call to fix something at one of those apartments, I did so with extra care, and I definitely watched my stuff. and I didn't figure it a surprise when Ms. Richards started suffering some illness, and her son suddenly became disabled. And her other son would die mysteriously in a couple of years. They were a targeted family.

So I was getting targeted terribly after the implant, and I was no longer able to really watch and take care of Janet like I normally did. Nor could I get back to my land at Jacksonville and enjoy the nearby beaches, so I sold it, and actually made a few thousand dollars from it.

Something bad was going to happen, and it did.

Disaster

"The Lord gave, and the Lord hath taken away. Blessed be the name of the Lord (Job 1: 21)."

It was all I could think of to say to a Pastor as I stood by and watched the west part of my house go up in flames. He stared icily ahead and said nothing, which I thought was just as weird.

I still have sorrow when I think about that day and how the perpetrators have sought to destroy everything I've worked for.

It wasn't much of a surprise to me when I came home that morning to find the street blocked off by emergency service crews. Like I said, I knew something was going to happen.

(Granted, whatever we think usually happens, but remember, I had been injected with something into my nervous system that dark morning in the back of my pickup truck at the Emerald Isle Fishing Pier, and I've really never been the same since. My equilibrium has been off since that time.)

I figured the fire was indeed at my house. I had built a fire in the woodstove that cold February morning for Janet to get warm, after I had picked her up from her ride letting her off from her nightly work at Harrah's casino.

So we had come home and sat around the stove. She then went to the bedroom to get some rest and I played some games on the computer. I then went off to a small job for a couple hours. I would have checked the stove on the way out to make sure everything was okay because I usually exit that door near the stove. But then I was getting targeted heavily.

Just a couple of weeks earlier, I had parked my truck at a convenience store, went in to get a snack, and come back out to see my truck rolling down the driveway. Fortunately, it hit a pole and stopped. It was a miracle no one got killed because there were a lot of cars pulling in and out of that parking lot.

Anyway, I do remember the fire was real hot, as I had put locust wood in that morning, and probably a big log so it would last until Janet got up.

But, I had warned Janet about the Christmas paper she had left near the stove months earlier, and I'm sure the paper was still there before the fire. I had not wanted to pester her again.

I came home to a shivering wife outside in the backyard with fire personnel spraying the west room addition with water. They were obviously influenced to do little else. I did not want to lose my house, so I told them to break in the front door and make sure the rest of the house was not burning. They did, but also sprayed water everywhere and did a lot of damage. Maybe I shouldn't have told them to break in the door. The fire had stopped, but smoke damaged the whole house.

The perpetrators had been getting in and out of the house where the addition was and they may have set the fire. I don't know. The fire chief tried to say flammables over on the counter were involved, but I don't think so. I found where the wood was charred directly behind the stove that showed an imprint of the ascending stove pipe. There was no protective cover there, as I had not installed one, and that was my fault,

But I had plenty of spacing between the wood wall and the stove, and I did not think there would be a problem.

Anyway, the house was in terrible shape – unlivable. The power company had cut the electric off for one thing, and it was freezing.

Janet and I stayed over her sister's that night, but all I could think about was my house, and I went over the next day to survey the damage. It was bad. Clothes and furniture were all ruined. The walls had black soot all over them. Plaster was peeling off the walls. The vinyl floor was blackened with smoke residue. The windows had a brown hazy oil over them that prevented sunlight from penetrating the room. Water from the fire hoses would sit in the corners of the rooms and begin to mildew the wood floors. All the kitchen cabinets were smoke damaged. All fixtures were blackened. And there was the acrid smell of petroleum and wood throughout the house.

I went out in the back yard which had a view of the street on the side. I sat down in what sunlight there was, against the stone wall against a bank of dirt I had built for flowers, and I just sat and cried.

Just shortly thereafter, Mrs. Foxx, one of Janet's in-laws, drove up, got out of the car, and walked to me. She had a meal in her hand and graciously gave it to me.

It was something I needed.

One of the neighbors helped me get all of the burnt stuff out of the addition. Tiles had popped up, and wood planks were strewn all over the floor, along with the metal roof panels that had fallen to the ground.

The only thing that survived the fire was a case of my books, *God's Help Now!*, sitting in the middle of the floor, with water all over the box and wet black ash. Incredible. Air couldn't get in the carton, so the books were okay.

I decided to get busy and rebuild, with or without Janet. I got the charred electrical circuits isolated and got the electricity turned back on and went to work. The first thing I did was put the appliances outside. They would all have to be cleaned.

About this time Janet's brother came over, walked in, looked at everything, and walked out. I had no help, which the programming does, so I knew I was on my own as I had been for forty years.

I ripped up all the vinyl flooring and the countertop covering and threw them away. All the clothing was put in the dumpster, for much of the synthetic materials had melted; the other was blackened.

It was eerie sleeping on the burnt wet floor in the bedroom the first few nights. The smell was horrific, but I was making progress, and then they tried to kill me again.

One night I was actually sleeping on the bed, when direct energy started hitting me. My internal organs started shaking about three in the morning. I was paralyzed with pain and fear, and all I could think to do was get off the bed and onto the floor. I shook for hours on the cold floor, and finally at dawn, I gathered myself enough to stand up and walk.

I continued with my work but I was definitely hurt. It took me weeks to recover. They tried to kill me that night. Upon research, I think they used infrasound to try and kill me. They can target bed springs, couch springs, and fixtures. That would be the last time I ever slept on a set of mattress springs, which act as antennas for their radiological assaults. But I tried it a couple of times later, and had some success, but the fact is the spring windings are being targeted for the energy. I've found the project programs behind the targeting and the radiological frequencies.

I had survived another attempt on my life. But I was very weak, and they would not stop trying to kill me. I sensed someone across the street was directing something at me, for when I made a concave reflection device – a man in nice dressed clothes suddenly took out from closed sliding glass doors in an abandoned house, ironically which was next to a hearing center.

And a man two doors down on the other side of the road would call me one day and ask a stupid question about how much it would cost to paint a ceiling. He was letting me know he was close by watching.

Anyway, in the house, I replaced all the windows, some doors, flooring, wall board, and painted everything three times. This took about a year, all the time while I was continuing to work my handyman job in the morning to try and make some money. But I was so used to adversity in my life; I just carried on.

I was exhausted and don't know where I got the strength to do all this work.

So making some progress from the February fire, the perpetrators made sure my July 4th holiday would be ruined, as I received divorce papers from Janet. I answered with a protective affidavit stating she had left me, just in case she tried to sue me for alimony.

The divorce, fire, and continual attacks on my life made me look for another life. I drove up to the main highway near the hospital, just a stone's throw from the house. I got out of the car, looked up and down the road, and prayed to God which way I should go. I was distraught from the divorce, the pain from working on the burned house for six months, and I was sick from the targeting. It was very lonely. And of course, Mom had passed away a couple years earlier.

I had little money since I had to spend quite a bit on the house. I was still working for the real estate company, and knowing I would need money to make another exit, I went out looking for things to do each morning at the rental houses, which was fine with the company.

Something had to change, and on one of my Sunday afternoon strolls on a bright sunny day, I looked up and down the nearby four lane road to ask for discernment about where I should go. I longed to get back to the ocean.

I had crossed this mountain twenty years ago. Now it was time to cross it again.

Wiser, more faithful, and more determined, I would survive these assaults and seek a happy life somewhere, and I would testify somehow of this torture and stalking. But as usual, my stalkers would follow me and seek to kill me several more times.

Going South

When I looked in my journal to continue this story, it was empty for the next five years, after another physical attack at the house.

I screamed out in torturous pain one night to Jesus for three days in the burned up house. The pain in my ears was similar to what I had experienced when I was 12 years old. Tears flowed for days with the pain. Somehow, they had again injected some microchips or whatever you want to call them in my ears again. It felt unusually full of something, so I knew something had happened. I understand they use some kind of gel that hardens into a receiver.

I wondered over the years, if the ear, nose, and throat doctor office on a neighboring street and the personnel inside had something to do with my attacks.

Right across the street on a hill is where I saw men scattering from a vacant house when I decided to reflect the energy back with a concave aluminum board. I must have guessed right about the direction.

The advent of the cell phone tower antennas only increased the problem, and many other victims are now complaining of electronic torture to their heads that is originating from remote locations.

I could not re-live the emotions of those years, until 2013 when I began to write this book again. I then had to stop for a couple more years until 2016. It has been too horrific to re-live.

Anyway, I traveled to the coast and found a nice private lot for sale twenty miles inland of the Myrtle Beach area -- in a neighborhood where there was good visibility – a primary consideration for a targeted individual.

The perpetrators have always tried to set up nearby so they can get to a house quick enough to drug foods, install cameras, and rearrange clothing to try and drive their victims crazy.

Traveling back to South Carolina to close the deal on some land a couple of weeks later almost got me killed again. The perpetrators did not want me moving.

I was traveling north on Route 701 approaching a crossroads about 60 miles per hour, only five minutes from the lawyer's office, when a huge utility truck kept creeping out in the road at the intersection. I thought he was just going to wait until I went by, but he kept inching forward and forward until he was near my lane!

I did not take any chances, knowing the perpetrators could have targeted the lineman (who still had his safety helmet on) with direct energy and confused him; so I slammed on brakes – and skidded off the road. I looked at him in disbelief, but there he was still inching across the road, by now, in my lane. I'm glad I stopped.

My real estate agent would not show up at the closing, which didn't surprise me.

I bought the land, met my new neighbor who sold it, and got busy looking for a mobile home to set up.

I had a septic tank installed on the lot, and upon the next trip, found a used mobile home for sale. It was ugly. The roof was uneven, mold was inside, and windows were cracked. It sat on the back of a trailer lot. But I only had so much money.

As I prayed over the matter, the Lord showed me the mobile home was on uneven ground. When leveled, the roof would level out. A good metal roof would prevent leaks, which I eventually installed.

Getting set up with my own place again in a nice area would be a major motivator for me after all I had been through. And now I realized who, how, and what the perpetrators were doing to me.

And I could get to the beach.

It was April and the water was warm enough to swim; I was in my environmental home.

Gone would be my mother who had passed away; Janet with her divorce, and the burned house.

After I purchased the trailer and got it moved to my lot, I went back to Sylva with a new outlook and hope. I just needed to get the Sylva house in livable shape, find a renter, subtly put my goods into boxes, and take off back to South Carolina.

Feeling some peace one night and having a little strength about 1:00 a.m., under the light of the moon, I packed my goods in the car and never looked back.

South Carolina

Crossing the state line for me became another blessing such as it did in 1989 going to North Carolina.

Watching the sun rise as I descended the mountains leaving North Carolina on I-26 gave me hope for peace, quiet, joy, and happiness.

But it doesn't seem to be possible to achieve such things as a targeted individual. The implants are in the head, and to try and remove them would invite disaster.

This reminds of the Biblical characters of faith in the Book of Hebrews, who knew they were strangers on earth but kept their focus on God's kingdom.

I was in very bad shape after the continual radiological attacks on my body at Sylva.

My face had lost its firmness because of the targeting. Subliminal songs continued to plague me, and I was exhausted. I was also penniless after purchasing the trailer, buying the land, and fixing up the house in Sylva.

But I did have help waiting for me.

I had met Barbara over the phone a month earlier as a reference from a work client, and she happened to live just 30 minutes from my lot.

She was a victim of this technology but in somewhat denial. The evidence and numbers surrounding her life were there however.

Anyway, she was a good soul, and I was blessed to have her as a friend. It did not surprise me when she said her husband was a former state trooper who had recently passed away. She described his death at home, and how he was unable to take care of himself though he was only sixty years old.

I made it as far as Marion when I just gave out; I lay out on the grass at a Wal-Mart parking lot.

Barbara met me there; bless her. We developed a close relationship and she helped me regain my strength by letting me stay at her house.

In my spare time, I went over to my trailer and started fixing it up, building a porch on the front, and doing lots of painting.

I did not want any electrical power due to my implants being activated. I used candles and flashlights for light, gas stoves for cooking and heat, and fixed a rain barrel under the guttering for water. That's how seriously affected I was from the neurotoxins in my body.

I lived like that most of the summer when I wasn't at Barbara's house.

And I had a job. Before I came to the coast, I started looking for jobs on the Internet. There were a few in the maintenance field, and after I was here a week, a Housing Authority hired me part-time.

But I could not get along with the lady boss, who was also part-time. She hated flowers! Imagine, a woman not liking flowers for the office.

After I brought some for the office one day, she removed them and put them in the kitchen!

But there were other problems as well. This Housing Authority was broke, and the State office had to assume temporary management. In fact, the town of Atlantic Beach itself was being investigated for being corrupt.

Looking to get closer to home and in a more stable position, I called a local apartment complex near home, and the maintenance man had just quit.

I was hired (after I recited the Apostle's Creed of all things). It was just a five minute drive from home. I stayed there five years and was blessed to have the greatest woman boss ever. She would bring me lunches at least once a week. She let me order the supplies I needed, handle all the maintenance repairing and contracting, and schedule my work as I pleased.

The perpetrators did not like this and tried to disrupt things several times, by using tenants to complain about unnecessary problems.

Mass programming the complex was taking place on Fridays for the tenants to complain and call about issues late in the afternoon. The programming went so far as to have a guy kick in the office door and set off firecrackers in the building and try to burn up the maintenance room on a July fourth evening.

After I repaired some items such as broken doors, key locks, toilets, and plumbing traps, the items would usually be messed up within a week by the perpetrators.

They used to clog the drains continually with chicken bones and food put in the toilet.

But for me, this was great job security, and I would get paid extra for going back and fixing things.

My boss decided to take some time off when her kinfolk came in town, and she called me at home excitedly on a Wednesday night telling me about their fun adventures.

But the next day, I received bad news from the part-time secretary, who was put in that position by the perpetrators: my boss had had a heart attack and died.

So, they killed her, and I know she was a targeted victim from her adopted childhood.

She was a wonderful loving person, and it took me a couple years before I really got over it.

In much of my spare time that first year here, I made my way to the beach to get sun and kill off the implants. The electrical pulsing bothered me terribly around the city area but I stuck it out and got better.

There were times on the beach when I would have to cover my neck with some foil to get relief, and I'm certain one day they tried to kill me with radiation from nearby. My heart was beating terribly fast, for an excessive period of time -- until I found a nearby piece of phosphate that I held on to for dear life so it would absorb some of the energy.

A victim friend and I years later would go to the beach one day. After about thirty minutes, each of us was getting a headache. Searching for the cause, there was a boat directly in front of us moored three hundred yards offshore. Unreal! Boats do not moor there just behind the breakers offshore!

When I pointed at the boat with the long antenna, they immediately pulled anchor and left. That didn't stop the perpetrators, as bright lights in the sky would follow us home, emanating some kind of energy trying to make us have an accident. Terre would have to grab a foil cover and put it in front of her while she drove. I just ducked.

Barbara and I would go many places discovering South Carolina, and we spent a week in Florida playing cribbage, visiting the parks, and making love at a nice resort. She claimed she was on some kind of hormone pills that kept her so active sexually, but I knew her targeting was probably stimulating her more than usual. Most victims complain of this. But this was fine with me in this stage of my life.

She also took some other doctor prescribed pills. Again, the targeting is designed to get people to buy pills. I asked her to reduce her dependency by at least by half in a year, because for one thing, she came extremely close to getting us into an accident on several occasions because of the effects she was experiencing from the pills. She had already told me she had been in a rollover accident a couple of years ago, and I didn't want it happening again. She drove mighty fast! And they would get her in a trance! I had never forgotten about the roll over incident. I asked her to get off the pills by one year.

It wasn't totally Barbara's pills taking that caused me to let her go. When I had received the vision to write *God's Help Now!* in 1988, there were illustrations in the book. But I could not find anyone to draw religious pictures. I had my book written and printed but no pictures.

The Lord would hold me to the task of putting pictures in this book! As much as I tried to avoid it, the mission was still there!

I also wanted to expand the devotional material with an Old and New Testament devotion for each of the seventy-one subjects. I had put all these thoughts in the back of my mind, because after all, I was still loaded with implants and still being stalked. The perpetrators would pull up newly planted trees at the house, break-in and drug the foods as usual, tear clothing, take stuff like tools and then replace them later. They would come in while I was sleeping and contaminate things. I finally had to block off my windows with panels, and that put a stop finally to the late night entries when I was asleep.

It got terribly lonely after breaking up with Barbara.

Victim Friends

One stormy evening under a full November moon, I went for a walk on the beach looking for valuables such as whelk shells, sharks' teeth, and sea glass, when I saw from the corner of my eye a woman approaching me from an angle.

Dressed in olive drab baggy pants, a long knitted scarf, woolen hat, and leather boots, she looked every bit of a victim out for a stroll.

She was attempting to gain in front of me and find sea gems first. I decided to compromise with this girl and see if we couldn't just search together. There was a lot of debris on the beach this evening after a storm.

I made conversation with her and we both loaded up on olive lettered, fossilized oyster shells, and clam shells, but then we came to a commercial crab trap, which I assume found its way from the Cherry Grove inlet out to the beach. Not a likely thing to pass up, and being the entrepreneurs we were, we looked at each other for a moment knowing it was going to take both of us to take it wherever.

It didn't take long to make a decision. We decided to take it up the beach near a house and hide it until we could get a vehicle and load it.

On the way back, she showed me her vehicle and we got in.

A bit of paranoia struck me after all I had been through, so I asked her, "You won't do anything to me, Will you?"

She said, "I'm supposed to say that."

Okay, I thought, *typical targeting answer.*

The perpetrators were using her to try and get at me but I was at least going to enjoy her company for awhile and go along with the ride.

I couldn't get her to understand about how her life was programmed, after she told me about unexplained sicknesses, a lump in her throat that caused indigestion, and her wrecked marriage.

She was always wanting to drag me off to a scam function, and she started making threatening remarks in the next couple of weeks.

I decided it was enough and left after a couple of months of seeing her. The programming will make people angry and aggressiveness for no good reason.

One day the perpetrators sent a girl in the water to swim with me. I had seen this girl reading a book on her lounge chair. She wasn't that pretty, but I knew something was amiss, especially when I gazed over at the cover of her book when I walked to the water: she was reading about colonial America and the Declaration of Independence.

Girls do not read that kind of book on a beach, unless of course they are history students in high school.

But this girl was in her middle twenties and she was an obvious trainee with some stalkers. Sure enough, I looked down the beach to see two young men gazing intently at us. I eventually swam off after she continued to ignore my questions. It was very strange. We were the only two in the water!

But I did have victim friends in the know. I had met them when I monitored the online petition. Jane lived near Raleigh. She claims she was implanted in the mountains of North Carolina near where I lived on a camping trip. She has marks to prove it, and she faithfully wrote a daily account of her targeting on the Internet. She was a kind soul and would invite me to stay at her house, especially around the holidays like

Thanksgiving. I would visit Jane, and she let me stay there when I went to card tournaments in Raleigh. This saved me money.

Staying with her in 2008 for a couple days made me realize it was time to get back into life. I had had no electricity and water for six months, living like a nomad. But my health had improved. Much of the black toxins had exited from my ears and other areas.

So I came home with renewed vigor shortly after Thanksgiving, especially after meeting one of Jane's friends and going out with her; however the perpetrators would knock her out with directed energy one night as we were romancing and playing a game.

I came home and dug in my water lines and installed my electrical disconnect box, pole, and wiring. Plus I got a well dug.

By Christmas, I had electricity and water. It's a good thing because it got very cold that next week, and all I had at that time was the electrical heaters I had brought from Sylva just in case I needed them.

For the want of companionship, I continued to get on the conference calls with other victims who were scattered across the United States and getting tortured. One girl, whom I'll call Charlene, was going to commit suicide somehow. She was in a St. Louis airport parking lot ready to end it. I told her to come here, and she came, driving the car with a pot over her head to protect her from the torture.

The perpetrators would target her terribly, and she would scream out in pain and cry. Sometimes she would just take off thinking things would get better and the targeting would lessen. Poor girl suffered terrible. Her head would swell with a knot, and there was a big lump on her forearm, which I presume were implants. She would only let me help her so much, for she was very paranoid. But we did have some fun, hanging around the beach, and going on drives.

She got some of her confidence back after a month and left. I encouraged her to leave, since she was getting better.

I could not support her financially. But I did enjoy her company. She came back a month later still wanting to hang around. I let her stay a couple days and then kicked her out. She was obviously just here to live free. I might add I got her started drawing Social Security first.

A couple more targeted individuals came by and stayed awhile, and the electronic targeting would try to separate us and make us argue. That's what the targeting does: pits Americans against each other. However, when you realize what's going on, you can deal with the adversity.

Many victims felt their prayers were going to be answered when President Obama created a Presidential Commission on Bio-ethics and conducted hearings by a panel of appointees: hundreds of victims promptly sent their stories of victimization off to the commission; they wanted to be heard.

I knew all along this was another attempt by the perpetrators to find out just who had the nerve to attend such a hearing, but many victims were allowed to testify. A video was made, and it was copied and put on the Internet.

I made a story out of the proceedings myself and put it on an independent news site, but it wasn't until one victim committed suicide that I did it.

Doris Anderson, (name changed for the sake of respect), who lived in California, went with a friend to a shooting range, and when her friend went to the bathroom, Doris pulled out a gun and killed herself. She had earlier complained she could no longer take the pain from the electromagnetic targeting. Her letter, just a couple of weeks earlier to the commission, was a plea for help, and it was ignored. I got a copy of the letter and included it in the news item. Bless her soul and may she rest in peace. She was a life-long victim.

After the deluge of victim stories at the second commission meeting (held quarterly), the commission members refused to hear further victim testimony – knowing that forced implant injections were being conducted by covert agencies to try and control innocent people with remote sensing equipment. The commission members were silenced.

Killing after killing has happened within the targeted individual community. Amanda, I think her name was, got on the conference call one night wanting to know just what we victims were experiencing. She had written a book or two on the brain, and she was writing another one. She had a doctorate degree in her field.

She gained much knowledge about how victims weren't sick at all, or mentally ill; they were being targeted electronically.

Amanda was dead three days later. The story goes that her car suddenly sped up on its own on a California road curve. She came up on another car in front of her and had nowhere to go – went over the guardrail and down the cliff where she died.

I had personally talked to her earlier that week.

Another victim, frantically asked for help on the calls, and had a couple of victims come down and stay at her house, but the targeting took over and they became distrustful of each other. Then she made the fatal mistake of renting a room out to a young man who was in denial of the targeting. Upon demanding some rent money a month later, the boy strangled her to death and set her house on fire.

This particular victim had complained of constant sexual stimulation (as many victims do), implants behind her eyes, and swellings on the head and breast areas.

Anyway, to keep busy and my mind off the targeting, I started an expanded version of *God's Help Now!* and called it *Devotions A-Z.*

With both Old and New Testament devotions for 71 subjects, I also put in pictures, using many pictures that Barbara and I had taken while traveling.

But the plane over-flights started increasing, break-ins to the trailer started occurring more, and the adverse energy worsened, especially at the apartment complex where I worked.

I've come home to torn clothes, stained papers, drugged foods, stolen paint and pesticide spray cans, and a load of other materials the perpetrators destroyed. One day both lines going to the toilets had been loosened and water was dripping on the rug.

Dealing with those incidents was common, as it had been for the last twenty years, but I was not able to deal with one that happened on Sunday afternoon when I let my guard down.

December 2, 2012, Drone Activity and Forced Drugging Murder Attempt

Drone aircraft began to fly over my trailer regularly on the weekends every hour or so beginning about October. Complaining to authorities did no good, and finally they accomplished their mission, keeping the area and me under surveillance for their forced drugging program.

On December 2, 2012, I found myself falling asleep in the living room. There was nothing I could do to stop the energy from making me tired.

I thought it was safe.

The drone airplanes and their electric motors were flying over the trailer all morning. I dozed off about 12:37 p.m. thinking everything would be alright.

But I awoke about 1:30 with signs of paranoia and tightness in my neck and fear that something dreadful had happened, especially after the subliminal words "anesthesia" during the morning.

The door was open, and I was scared to death.

My mouth was dry. My forehead felt as if someone had scraped away my nerve endings. And there was an empty feeling in my head, especially in the front part of the forehead area. The feeling was gone.

This time it was serious, so I went and looked for some clay to ingest to stop it, but it was in my bloodstream, and I tried some charcoal to no avail.

I couldn't think, and I lay listlessly on the floor knowing they had poisoned me again.

All the neighbors had been gone, and these perpetrators often attack on Sundays. Always have, and especially around the Thanksgiving holidays.

After a couple of days, I came to my senses:

It took me weeks to get some real thought back – the micro-chips blocking the blood flow to my head.

And I had just mentioned a few days earlier to a friend down at the beach how my nervous system was finally relaxing and the particles were coming out, after years of suffering.

I know the perpetrators heard me for sure.

This neurotoxin had gone straight to my brain to kill me, and to my optic nerve to impair me.

I now have all kinds of spots in my vision, the ringing in my ears louder than ever, and all kinds of black stuff around my ears.

They've destroyed my life -- all in an attempt to disable me, steal my equity, and defame my reputation.

Maybe it's all because of two lawyers trying to hold onto their reputations from 1986.

But many victims think, *They have taken out life insurance policies on us.*

It was a year before I could drive in traffic at the beach because there was so much fluid in my head fighting off the toxins.

I have in my notes: *three months later I am still sickened, but some of the polymer substances are coming out from around my face. I contacted several lawyers about this situation. One wanted a $50,000 retainer.*

Another lawyer asked me why the CIA was picking on me. I told him the MK-Ultra documents say they are attacking Native Americans and unwitting victims.

Drone activity immediately ceased after the attack.

But I'm glad I called and complained, because shortly thereafter a bill passed the State Senate forbidding drones from gathering personal information from private citizens. I guess the lawyers understood what happened and got scared.

Seeing that I wasn't dead or visiting the cancer center with all my implants, the perpetrators programmed an accident to happen that was near deadly about a year later.

On a Friday evening, a bicyclist had been killed by a vehicle just outside of town, and, police were out taking measurements and investigating the scene the next morning, but they only had one blue safety light twirling above a patrol car sitting in the middle of the road.

I was heading out to play golf, and figuring I was in no hurry, decided to sit and wait it out, like one other car ahead of me.

I was a bit tired anyway from Friday night's targeting.

After a couple minutes, I looked in my rear view mirror to see a car coming straight at me at 50 mph and not slowing down.

I had no time to do anything but duck and brace myself against the floorboard and seat back, and I just knew I would be dead or severely injured.

I don't remember anything of the impact, but the driver of the oncoming car must have stepped on the brakes at some point because I was still alive only 65 feet down the road on the left.

He had hit the rear right side of my car, and the back windshield had flown up to the front seat, and the trunk was smashed nearly to the back windshield.

But I was alive. My back and knee hurt, but I thanked God I was alive.

So I got out, limped around a bit to see if I could walk, and then went back to get my camera.

I figured this was a programmed event, and sure enough, the license plate read 293, which is a perpetrator targeting number. You will see this number often during the targeting events (plane accidents, etc . . .). This is real. I've mentioned the 6 upside down.

It's a good thing I took pictures because the policeman who finally showed up about an hour later failed to record just where my car was after it was hit.

Then the tow truck wanted $250.00 to tow my car just a few miles, but he was obviously in agreement with the patrol officer, and what choice did I have.

Now I was really frightened to drive, still trying to recover from the toxin attack and now this, but somehow I was able to drive a rental car and make it through the next month until I got my car. And the rental car driver understood why I was bracing myself against the dashboard when she exceeded the speed limit.

Evil did not stop: the perpetrators tried to buy off one attack, putting $2,000 in an envelope in a used book at the library.

I had gone to the discarded book shelf as I do occasionally to check out the latest deals: I found some books had just been put there about golf.

I opened one to find a creased envelope in the back of the book where a person could not miss it.

I actually thought it might be some additional instructional material. A bit curious and not wanting it to fall out, I put it in my pocket. I was going to get the book anyway.

As I grabbed the book, two women pretended to browse the shelves for a book just a few feet away to see if I got the book.

One was sitting on the floor, the other standing beside her, and they were obviously perpetrator conspirators confirming my actions to get the book.

Just in case they were co-conspirators, I turned to put the envelope in my pocket, slipped the book under my arm, and went to the checkout desk to buy it.

Once in my car, I put the envelope on the sun visor and forgot about it.

But opening the sealed envelope a couple of weeks later revealed 20 crisp one hundred dollar bills in an envelope.

The perpetrators had tried to get me to open the envelope earlier as I drove by an electronic messaging sign near Route 57 on the way to the beach, for a message flashed: "Put the money in the bank."

So what was the money for? Possibly because to get rid of implants I sunbathe naturally in a private room, it helps kill off some toxins. So maybe the perpetrator was filming or something. I don't know.

I thought maybe I had left the torturers back at Sylva until when I came home to the trailer one day and started cleaning out the cabinets – only to find items that were missing for nearly seven years suddenly appear. This has to be one obsessed individual to hold onto a person's private property for that long.

The Killing Program

I cringe when I hear of another murder by the three six computer generated killing program.

At some point in the future, this is all going to be exposed. People think I'm off my rocker suggesting these randomized frequencies produced by electronic means are causing terrible things to happen, but the evidence is prevalent.

Robin, one of the first victims I had ever talked to about ten years ago, called me on Friday night. She carried on about the perpetrators stealing body parts and killing people. Robin is trying to inform the public also. She's been on talk radio shows and the Internet, and her perpetrators can't shut her up as much as they've raped and poisoned her. She's one awesome woman who displays raw human emotion of sympathy, pain, and love for the people, especially children.

I may have failed to mention, but the first victim I met after I wrote the petition was a girl who swore these perpetrators were coming in at night and stealing her eggs.

I contacted one girl who wrote a book about her father's mission to preach in a small North Carolina town, where the family was terrorized for years. And her mother was killed. The young girl lived through it, but never really saw the originator of all the evil. The three six numbers surrounding her mother's killer tipped me off.

The essence of her book is to find forgiveness through Jesus for the offensive evil acts of people. But this targeting system is not an object for forgiveness: the programmers and anti-Christ groups are guilty. They just use simple people to carry out their mission: destroy people of faith.

The perpetrators drove her father to suicide, getting him to hear voices and also to be impotent. They had it out for him in the beginning, because he was preaching the word of God.

Ironically, that story took place just twenty-five miles from where I live.

A three-year old child was tortured in "Marlboro" county, with "cigarette burns" to her genitals. This is the nature of what this targeting system does to uninformed people – make a cartoon of torture applications to human psyches. And law enforcement and the media don't always understand.

It's really simple enough to find out if you are victim of this electronic targeting, by just crinkling up some aluminum foil and putting it near the side of the head or throat area, where you might feel pain. The perpetrators have put an implant in my throat area that is highly sensitive to some kind of low frequency emanation. They usually torture this area at 3:00 in the afternoon, just after dinnertime, or around 7:00 in the morning. The pain pulses down into the chest area, but the foil nearly stops it.

There are more death incidents that have commonalities, like three important people who died from drowning in a span of two days: one a lawyer on vacation in the Caribbean islands, another woman who was practicing diving off the South Carolina coast who never made it back to the boat, and a union negotiator who had just finalized a contract with communications' workers drowned at a North Carolina island.

Then three tragic accidents involving young people occurred near here; one woman was hurried to pass an ambulance on the right side on the grass running over a bystander.

These accidents, in my opinion, are programmed. When the numbers come together, such as road addresses, ages, and calendar dates, targeting is taking place and unwitting people are getting caught up in unsafe situations.

A considerable amount of people have run off an otherwise safe country road to their deaths. The road number? Highway 66.

And just recently, a good plumber friend of mine was run over in the road and died. Sure he might have been more attentive, but the programmed radiation fields are distracting people.

God has revealed much to me about the targeting: why plastic drink bottles have different swirling patterns on them, why can goods have different rings around their lids and bottoms, or why everyday wear jeans have metal rivets with circles on them, all designed to let the system know what is being used when targeted with the energy. It's that bad.

I caught on one day when I opened a "green giant" can and heard subliminally the jolly green giant song. And then I saw the definitive rings on the can lid.

For years I wondered about a cowlick on top of the head, only to find out hair was pushed up by an implant in the region; but a strong magnet was able to take care of that and burned up the implant.

If it had not been for my faith -- and my knowledge of herbs, I'd be gone. One thing that saved me time and again was the use of charcoal as an anti-oxidant.

Stealing My Future

The battle continued as I had to fight for my retirement pay. Where other people just apply and get theirs in 30 days or so, I had been waiting over two years. At the time of this first writing, I was only getting a portion of what I was supposed to be getting. I had to file legal briefs in two judicial proceedings.

Not only did the Office of Personnel Management fail to give me my full retirement but tried to extort money from me saying my employer failed to make deposits on my behalf (in violation of 5 U.S.C. 8334)!

Absent finality, I went to the U.S. District Court in Florence, South Carolina and filed suit to protect myself.

They disclaimed immediate jurisdiction, so after I received a final determination of benefits from OPM, I filed an appeal with the Merit Systems Protection Board, who would also disclaim jurisdiction! I filed a Petition for Rehearing.

Who on earth has jurisdiction over corrupt federal government proceedings?

And my retirement file at home would be missing! It had been stolen by the perpetrators. So I had to request copies from archive centers.

Now I know why I never got the Postmaster job I worked so hard to get. Nor did I get full-time maintenance worker jobs I was more than qualified for after I had worked for the National Park Service for years

That's the life of a targeted individual. And I hope you never become one.

But the problem is that cell phone tower antennas, microwave repeaters, ground wave antennas, and the HAARP system are all affecting the populace. The transmissions are only increased with the aluminum in the air from military spraying. And it's obviously coordinated with the medical community somehow, because the spraying nearly always occurs at the end of the month when most people get funds – so they will go spend it for prescription drugs.

Radiological pollution is the biggest threat to mankind. With more additives in foods and the air, which are contributing to transmit artificial sound and disturbance to the nervous system, humanity will suffer.

I went out and played golf one Monday and thought the perpetrators were going to cripple me. There was a cell phone tower right at the putting green at one of the back nine holes, and energy started hitting all my bones to where I could barely walk. I had been playing here before and never got bothered as such, but this was serious. I told the other players I was in pain and to go ahead and play; then I was able to finish playing the hole, but my primary thought was to get off the green and behind the trees on the way to the next teeing area to get some relief. Every bone joint in my body was hurting, and I knew I was being targeted somehow from the tower antenna. This particular course does have some kind of a GPS monitoring ability for the players and each hole on the course. Finally, the further I got away from the tower, the pain started to go away, which I thought would happen. I'll never go there again.

Prayerfully, a pact between all countries will be made that limits artificial radiation, identifies the sources, and warns the public of the danger. This will happen at some point but not until many people will suffer and complain, probably similar to the epidemic from cigarettes giving people lung cancer.

The victims of targeting know what is happening and stories like this one are warning the public to take action now. Lives are being ruined by these injections of neuro-toxins. In some cases, a whole life span has been ruined such as mine, because the toxins are so deep and biologically inert, so they can't be found.

But God knows and the perpetrators will be held accountable for the millions of people that have died unnecessarily as a result.

I came across a victim friend the other day, who I reached out to a couple years back, and she was nearly in tears. She had quit her job claiming she was lied to and defamed by her boss. Her crops at home suddenly weren't growing any longer. And she had thoughts of craziness.

This is what the program does to people, and it must be stopped.

As I'm updating this book here in 2021, a few things have changed. I finally got my full retirement pay, thanks to Senator Graham. I've published a new devotional booklet yearly called *Quiet Heavens.*

And I've stopped working a regular job.

But every day, I scrape off black polymer type substances from my legs, neck, arms, feet, and facial areas.

Yet, God is faithful, and I'm still actively exposing the most heinous crime ever of remote sensing and targeting people to commit violence and have their mental health impaired.

Until this surveillance system is eliminated, mass shootings, illness, and chaos will continue. Lately I've been documenting extraordinary numbers of animals dying after nights of chem.-trail spraying.

All radiation media should be insulated; otherwise, humans and animals will suffer the consequences.

May God have mercy on us.

Kenneth M. Lee 2021

Printed in the USA
CPSIA information can be obtained
at www.ICGtesting.com
LVHW010154050424
776520LV00008B/328